# RAT REBELLION

ONYE KINGSLEY

Dedicated to the children and people of Africa, whose lives and future have been blighted, bruised and battered by the actions and inactions of men in high places.

Order this book online at www.trafford.com/07-0632
or email orders@trafford.com

Most Trafford titles are also available at major online book retailers.

Note for Librarians: A cataloguing record for this book is available from Library and Archives Canada at www.collectionscanada.ca/amicus/index-e.html

Printed in Victoria, BC, Canada.

ISBN: 978-0-9569415-2-7

*We at Trafford believe that it is the responsibility of us all, as both individuals and corporations, to make choices that are environmentally and socially sound. You, in turn, are supporting this responsible conduct each time you purchase a Trafford book, or make use of our publishing services. To find out how you are helping, please visit www.trafford.com/responsiblepublishing.html*

*Our mission is to efficiently provide the world's finest, most comprehensive book publishing service, enabling every author to experience success. To find out how to publish your book, your way, and have it available worldwide, visit us online at www.trafford.com/10510*

www.trafford.com

**North America & international**
toll-free: 1 888 232 4444 (USA & Canada)
phone: 250 383 6864 ♦ fax: 250 383 6804
email: info@trafford.com

**The United Kingdom & Europe**
phone: +44 (0)1865 722 113 ♦ local rate: 0845 230 9601
facsimile: +44 (0)1865 722 868 ♦ email: info.uk@trafford.com

10 9 8 7 6 5 4 3 2

# ACKNOWLEDGEMENTS

THE AUTHOR would like to thank the following people: my parents, Chief Anthony Onyekwuluje and Chief (Mrs) M Nnwayimgbo Onyekwuluje, for giving me the best education, which fired my creative talents; my beautiful wife, Chioma; other members of my family; G Jill Todd Cert Ed., DipPRE of GJT Editing and Proofreading Services for her hard work and the staff of Trafford Publishing, without whom this thought-provoking novel would not have seen the light of day.

Thanks to you all.

# PREFACE

R AT REBELLION is a compelling satirical novel, intelligently and graphically written, with symbols and anecdotes depicting the economic and sociopolitical state of affairs that prevail in some African and other Third World countries, represented by the fictional City of Canterborne. The title, Rat Rebellion, metaphorically means 'the rebellion of the oppressed people', so one could call it the 'people's rebellion'.

This is a novel depicting corrupt leaders and how they view their subjects as rats that are only good to be used, dumped and trampled upon – 'in their mind's eye the masses only exist to be exploited and trampled upon as rats'.

The humans are the privileged class, the upper and ruling class with their numerous cronies and family members. Some relatives are poor and neglected, being treated like distant relations whilst the affluent wallow in their wealth and riches. Mayor Dan Dakota, Mayor O'Brien, their cabinet ministers, hangers-on and family members represent the human leaders of Canterborne.

The rats are the poor, deprived downtrodden citizens of Africa living in the City of Canterborne. They are the underdogs, the underprivileged, the common man on the street, the working class. Their friends and families are in greater numbers, the majority of the electorate whose votes put the humans into power, which is now used to exploit them. The rats make up the oppressed majority of the teeming population of Canterborne and her numerous localities scattered abroad. The Jungle Rat Community is led by Konky, the rats' mercenary in wartime. The vivid rat characters voice that which is in the minds and thoughts of both the oppressors and the oppressed. They can be very mischievous, their only way of exacting retribution on the ruling class and their entourage, and preparing for what is to come.

The author's repeated use of 'Mr' and 'Mrs' depicts equality, dignity and respect, showing that all the characters are human beings and it is only their position in the corrupt society of the day that marks the difference.

Rat Rebellion graphically exposes and presents the degree and magnitude of the general maltreatment, poverty, insecurity, double standards, deprivation, gross level of abuse and loss of life faced by the rats. It also exposes how they have been abandoned by those whom they voted into power. There are various levels of oppression and conflicts, even among the rats, symbolised by other animal predators. The irony of it all is that even within the same circle, some of the underprivileged still oppress others, but not on the same scale as the leadership of the day.

Rat Rebellion is set in the small village of Cayon, and later the City of Canterborne, in Mayor O'Brien's bakery on the outskirts of the city.

Sacks and bags of cereals symbolise the nation's natural resources, which are beyond the reach of the common man in society and are usually only enjoyed by the corrupt leaders of the day, their cronies and families. To wreak revenge on the leaders, the rats had to steal and vandalise the resources, 'ripping the bags and sacks of cereals' amongst other things.

*

One wonders about the end result. What could happen eventually if things get out of hand? At the end of the day people say true power lies with the electorate, but could this be true in the case of Rat Rebellion? I wonder!

# CHAPTER ONE

DAN DAKOTA, the mayor of the City of Canterborne, was a man noted for his arrogance, meanness and decisiveness, who would stop at nothing to get what he wanted, ready to do the unspeakable to satisfy his desires. He was the type who would make you an offer you would be nuts to decline. The rats and human citizens of the city disliked him, for he had sweet-talked them into voting for him in the election and in some quarters it was rumoured that he had conned his way into becoming the mayor by way of a rigged election. He was hard on the people and a terror to the world of teeming rats who resided in Canterborne.

In the early days, Mr Rodent and other rats were secretly living in Mr O'Brien's bakery. It was during Dan Dakota's term of office that Mr Rodent began making plans for his future and that of his generation. It was a kind of wake-up call for him and others who shared his vision, so he began a furtive rat mobilisation and awareness campaign. He thought about the future of his fellow rats, and finally came to the reasoned conclusion that they should start something, at least on a small and quiet scale, which would eventually grow from there.

One of his major roles was to station six smart mice in and around the household of Mayor Dan Dakota, the first three to spy within his living quarters, two in his office and one permanently stationed in his official car, the one he used most often. Their major role was to eavesdrop and relay all relevant information to Mr Rodent at the Bakery Rat Community, acting as his eyes and ears.

Mr Rodent pointed out:

"This system will ensure that we are well ahead and privy to plans and situations beforehand as it affects the rat community. We will then have contingency plans to beat his system if we can."

Mr Rodent was a young smart rat, leader of the rat community residing in Mr O'Brien's small bread making industry. He and others had nicknamed the place the 'Bakery Rat Community' to the envy of the Jungle and Storage Rats' Communities.

Mayor Dan Dakota could hardly be caught out on anything. One minute he was an angel and the next, the red-horned devil himself doing the unspeakable. Occasionally he had to cover his tracks with bloodshed; the killing and maiming of his political rivals and anyone unlucky enough to renege or flout his beliefs. Staying in power was all that really mattered to him and possibly his only reason for living.

He once wiped out the entire family of his closest friend, Rocky Otelo, simply because he had attended a press conference with the national news media and the views he expressed were very contrary to his own. To Dan, that was the first sign of disloyalty and betrayal, which had to be dealt with to drive home his point. By the time the interview was over, he had detailed his special killer squad to visit his friend's family and annihilate them all with no exception. Even Nelson, his friend's six month old baby, was murdered in cold blood to teach Rocky Otelo a lesson he would never forget. On returning home, Otelo was horrified to see the carnage, but he immediately got the message and knew that he had to flee Canterborne without delay if he was to see the next sunrise.

The mayor blamed loose canon gangs of reckless armed bandits for the heinous crime. He said he had assembled a ' strong team of his combined forces of police and military men to investigate the dastardly attack and bring the perpetrators to account, with the promise that justice would prevail as soon as they were apprehended. Those who watched the news item were busy hailing Dakota's commitment to the issue, but the truth was he never allowed an independent investigation of the case to take place and refused to release funds needed for an inquiry. As a result, the case sunk into oblivion, leaving Rocky Otelo to begin life afresh in a foreign land.

The mayor ensured that he had enough money to cover his tracks through bribery and corruption. He had a finger in every dubious pie, making certain that numerous storage facilities were built so that surplus money was always available to lavish on himself, his cronies, friends, their families and those who showed him loyalty. Absolute loyalty was paramount in Dakota's camp if one was lucky enough to be one of the favoured few. Mr Bamby, one of his loyal supporters said, 'Who pays the piper dictates the tune'.

Dan Dakota ordered dozens of storerooms to be constructed, each one with rat-proof specifications, each containing a specific type of cereal and each one situated quite a distance from the next. What he did not know was that some small groups of rat families still managed to eke out a living at his expense. Life for these rats was dull, dry and boring because of the lack of variety, which in some ways is the spice of life.

"Waking up each morning and feeding on the same kind of meal day in, day out, is certainly not my idea of fun," said Mr Spicy, one of the young vibrant rats residing in one of the storerooms. "It's a nightmare living here. I honestly think nowhere could be better to live than the

Bakery Rat Community," he concluded, playing with the tail of Parcey, his girlfriend.

Mr Parotty was Mayor Dan Dakota's communications secretary. He was a man of many parts, and among his amusing and curious antics was the inability to speak the truth. He thought that 'black is never black and white is never too white'.

"Everything can usually be twisted around to suit your whims. In life people often dislike the truth because it is a bitter pill to swallow, but colour the situation with the addition of sugar or even honey and, believe me, you'll become loved and everyone will be running after you," Parotty would often say to his close junior colleagues.

He was never short of words to explain away whatever he and the mayor had decided to take on, for they thought and acted as one in most cases.

"Keeping Mr Parotty in my cabinet was one of the best decisions I have ever made. It is like always having some-one to cover your back and your dirty deeds even when you are not looking," Dakota continually boasted.

# CHAPTER TWO

THE RESIDENTS of the City of Canterborne were shocked to the core and brought to their knees when, by some miraculous circumstance, the financial storage accounts headquarters, a huge seven-storey building, was torched and raised to the ground by a faceless arsonist. Tension was high and some suggested an accounts cover-up, but no one dared to voice the name of their suspect for fear of reprisals.

In recent times Canterborne had been a hotbed of financial looting of oil profits and gross mismanagement of the nation's wealth, to which those at the top claimed no responsibility and passed the buck. This building being burned was altogether something different, and tongues were secretly wagging all over the city. Everyone guessed practically the same, but no one dared to speak out loud enough to be heard. Mayor Dan Dakota had succeeded in putting the fear of God into everyone with his ruthlessness.

The mayor promptly set up a special investigation squad to look into the matter, and Mr Parroty jumped at the opportunity to rescue his boss and explain away the disaster as a terrible miscalculation of a disgruntled arsonist, the handiwork of Dakota's political enemies and detractors who were desperate to get even with him and ruin his good works. To drive home his point, the mayor invited the nation's news media and the TV networks to witness a public display of lorry loads of countless, empty burned gas cylinders, jerry cans of fuel and even bundles of lighters and matches. His men claimed these items were found in the basement of the incinerated building by an investigating team.

"These are the devices used by our detractors to bring our good reputation into disrepute," Dan Dakota said.

At the end of the day opinions were divided on the issue, which later died a natural death. Not a shred of any accounting evidence was ever seen, as all the documents had gone up in smoke leaving behind a badly burned building, once the pride of the nation's petroleum resources accountability, but now a ghost of its former glory.

A few months later, the promise of rebuilding the building with the proceeds of another successful oil exploration venture, was made, however, this did not draw much applause from either the human or rat communities of the City of Canterborne. Some intelligent residents knew exactly what had happened, but no one was foolhardy enough to speak their mind and risk a certain journey to an untimely death and the graveyard where several unmarked graves bore the ludicrous epitaph – may your soul rest in peace. This was fast becoming a commonplace occurrence.

In the Bakery Rat Community, Mr Rodent and his fellow rat leaders had first-hand knowledge of what had happened because of the daily reports and feedback from the secret spy mice scattered around Mayor Dakota's location. They eavesdropped on his furtive conversations and plans, some hearing of the arson plan the day before the fire. They were politically and financially powerless to nip the plans in the bud, so tended to look away to avoid suspicion or serious attack after the event.

They knew the rat population was still far below the

expected target and the Bakery Rat Community was still in its formative years. They did not want to give anything away, not yet, for there would be time enough for that, so they bided their time, calmed down and did not give the game away.

"There is sense in waiting," opined Mr Rodent.

The spy mice were extremely smart and effective, making sure they were in the right place at the right time, but avoiding suspicion, especially in the daytime when humans could see clearly. They attached themselves securely beneath Mayor Dakota's large, multicoloured woollen sofas very close to the corners of his lounge for easy escape if the need arose. Hanging there silently, they listened and sifted the mayor's current news, plans and secret agendas appertaining to the City of Canterborne, which he discussed with his men and cronies.

The rats' community survival depended on having a first-hand briefing of whatever the mayor and his followers were plotting as regards their livelihood in the city. It was imperative that they were well aware, ahead and abreast of any situation that could be adjusted to aid their survival in Canterborne.

"We hate surprises in the Bakery Rat Community and cannot afford the costs," Mr Rodent pointed out to one of his spy mice, encouraging him to make sure all facts and information were accurate and not the opposite as had been the case a few weeks previously.

Dan Dakota, the mayor of the City of Canterborne, often saw the city as his personal estate and likewise every human, material and natural resource in the land. He believed he had absolute power to do things and get away with them, as did his cronies who were often the brains behind most actions.

"You play the game as it comes, but you must win at all times, even if you have to turn back the hands of the clock," the mayor often stressed, for he liked nothing better than to have permanent friends or enemies.

Dakota did not believe in caring for the inhabitants of the various resource locations within the city and certainly did not believe in ploughing back some of the profits for developmental purposes. His only concern was the exploitation of resources in any way he could and in whatever manner he saw fit to meet his selfish and endless desire for a better and more extravagant and high-class lifestyle for himself and his cronies.

The human and rat community members of the City Of Canterborne can go to hell. They might as well return to the thick forests and rural areas if they want to, Dakota thought.

Mr Magade Robot, Dakota's political advisor, was usually responsible for major issues of the day in the City of Canterborne. For reasons best known to himself, he had led the campaign to sack the farm owners of Maloney district, fertile agricultural land in the south-east of the city. He eventually succeeded in sacking and seizing their land, produce, homes and livestock; those who had been the food basket for Canterborne for ages. Some said Robot did this to impress the voters for the second term election.

The human and rat citizens of Canterborne were sick, homeless and starving as a result of Mr Magade Robot's decisive actions without proper consultation. There was no reasonable alternative in place to provide a livelihood for them. He had to contend with several pockets of opposition scattered among the people, and the situation degenerated into indiscriminate arrests, prosecution, imprisonment, and the killing and maiming of innocent citizens by controlled military and police forces.

Paul Kwesi, a commercial city taxi driver who openly criticised the leadership of the day as being insensitive and barbaric in handling issues, was overheard by one of the mayor's secret agents. He never returned home, for he was promptly arrested and imprisoned for carelessly exercising his freedom of speech, which had suddenly become a taboo in the city run by Mayor Dan Dakota and his loyal followers.

It became an all too familiar sight to see citizens stretched out lying face downwards in the street receiving corporal punishment from the mayor's special squad for speaking their minds about the government's policy affecting their lives. As a result of this brutality, thousands left their beloved City of Canterborne in droves, in search of greener pastures elsewhere and abroad.

- In Mayor Dakota's government there was no hope or cause to salvage the nation's economy. Civil servants in essential positions were dissatisfied as a result of delayed salaries and poor pay packets. To make matters worse, the judicial system was equally affected, with judges not being given the opportunity to perform fairly, their decisions being interfered with to the point that they were instructed whom to free, jail or condemn. Even the lawyers were made out to be untruthful, and had to twist the constitution, interpreting the law to suit the government of the day.

In the midst of this mayhem, Mr Magade Robot was busily scheming. Everything in life meant politics, even football matches and cricket games were exploited for political attention. He would not leave any stone unturned to ensure that the next election was won, so that they would remain in power to continue their 'good work', as he often said.

At the Bakery Rat Community, Mr O'Brien struggled with his bread making business, having recently located to the City of Canterborne with his wife and Anita, their daughter. It was hard work running the business singlehandedly, and things were far from good. He worked extremely hard very late into the night, trying to meet the demands and satisfaction of his increasing number of customers. He really did not mind about the growing rat population in his little factory because they were all keeping quiet and out of sight. They often remained in their dark hiding places until very late at night when Mr O'Brien was exhausted enough to retire for the day.

Mr Rodent and the others were wise enough to keep well hidden until Mr O'Brien went to bed in the adjoining room then they could roam freely, looking for food and meeting friends and families in the bakery community.

It was common knowledge that Mr and Mrs Messy's family were always arguing and never seemed to stop all night; a rather incompatible family unit. Mrs Messy seemed to expect certain miracles from her husband, Mr Sam Messy. She required perfection at all times, which he agreed was beyond his capabilities, so he tried to coast along with her just to save their marriage. He had no idea what surprises were in store for him as nothing was pre-planned.

Mr Rodent had a wonderful family and enjoyed sharing his time with them despite his very busy schedules in the Bakery Rat Community where everyone always seemed to be complaining about something. At times he took a quiet holiday with the family, often visiting the jungle rat families, especially his friend Mr Konky, who doubled as a personal friend and also his brother-in-law. Visits to him relieved the family of the stress that was often the severe price to pay for being a leader of a very complex community.

# CHAPTER THREE

Mr o'brien's bakery business was starting to pick up and he now had a staff of two working for him. He was thinking of possible expansion on the same site, for he needed more space for storage rooms and his night staff. To achieve his goal he had to work even harder, being an industrious man who believed in himself and his demanding work.

"My hard work will get me there!" he once told one of his business customers, who was encouraging him to expand his business and employ additional staff.

After a few months when the dream had become a reality, 'My hard work will get me there' instantly became a regular statement, almost a motto, for Mr O'Brien's staff, who adopted his saying as their message of inspiration for success.

When one of the bakery workers brought a dog to live there it soon terrorised the rat community and became the death knell for entire families. It dragged innocent rats from their homes to please its owner, and word travelled around the bakery that a terrible and merciless predator was on the loose. Those who could not weather the storm relocated to the nearby jungles and forests in large numbers rather than pay the supreme price of losing their lives.

Junta the dog was so ruthless that he derived pleasure in sniffing out every burrow in the bakery in the hope of annihilating any family still at home. He barked and scratched at the entrance to try to get in, and those not brave enough to withstand this obvious threat often made a quick dash for it right into his path, only to be killed instantly. As a result, hundreds lost their precious lives in this way, and there was no respite from the vicious attacks, for every day Junta became more devious in his search.

It was all getting out of hand, so Mr Rodent summoned a senior Bakery Rat Community meeting and demanded that they should all wake up and do something about the dog before everyone was killed.

"This is a dog that has refused to mind its own business ever since Mr John brought it into the bakery community to live with him. What shall we do now?" Mr Rodent asked.

No one had an answer to this tortuous question and eventually they all dispersed as quietly as they had arrived. After an interminable week of clandestine meetings, which yielded no result, most of the dwindling rat community felt that all hope was lost, and planned to relocate to the nearest jungle to start a new tough life.

Quite unexpectedly, out of the blue came Mr Nutty, a smart young maverick of the community who was extremely exasperated with the terrible game of hide-and-seek. He feared losing his lovely home in the Bakery Rat Community to the 'bully Junta', as he often called the marauding dog. It was Mr Nutty who finally came up with a suggestion to which everyone, including Mr Rodent, agreed.

"Anything is worth doing to get rid of Junta the terror dog," said Mr Rodent.

Everyone was surprised when Junta was found lying helpless, gasping for breath on the pavement a few weeks later. He had eaten a poisoned dead rat Mr Nutty had dragged in from the humans' neighbourhood in the middle of the night and placed at the entrance to a burrow frequented by the dog. Junta finally died in the early hours of the morning and everyone was over the moon. Some guessed at how Mr Nutty had managed to perpetrate the deed, but all agreed that it was an act of extreme bravery, and they were overjoyed and relieved.

Every rat began to think where it would all end. It was another wake-up call to the rat leaders of the Bakery Rat Community to look to the future and make plans.

At each cabinet meeting, Mayor Dakota talked about fashioning a home-grown democracy for his people. Some City of Canterborne residents wondered what had happened to the true democracy of the civilised world, and questioned why some leaders and citizens hid away behind closed doors to fashion a so-called home-grown democracy.

When a spy mouse overheard a conversation on this subject he reported back to Mr Rodent.

"This is a massive psychological fraud on the deprived human and rat citizens of the City of Canterborne. Home-grown democracy, my foot! Why should anyone in their right mind run away from the rest of the civilised world only to hide under the ludicrous canopy of home-grown democracy, which means nothing but a perpetuation of his evil rule on us all?" said Mr Rodent, his voice cracking with anger. "I seize this opportunity to further encourage my fellow rats to step up our numbers by massive procreation."

He knew that the secret of their power lay in numbers and the larger their population the better chance of survival they would have.

"There is sense in numbers," Mr Rodent concluded.

# CHAPTER FOUR

NEW DISCOVERY of additional natural resources, especially in oil and petroleum products, were emerging daily from new locations in the oil-rich and wealthy landmass of the City of Canterborne, but the equal distribution of the benefits was nothing to write home about. Humans, and especially the rat communities, whose private property generated this wealth were systematically denied the basic necessities of life like potable water, shelter, food and good roads. Mr Jeremy Timber, a middle-aged rat citizen, narrated the woeful tale of how his family land had been forcefully taken away under the mayor's leadership with little or no compensation.

A few weeks later there was a terrific blast - vandalism of the oil pipelines by some faceless young rats who were resource control protesters. This led to massive oil spillages that eventually covered the farm settlements and produce, killing human and rat citizens, and destroying rubber plantations, and cocoa and palm trees in Niogo, a town in the southern part of the City of Canterborne. Starvation threatened everyone. The population was driven farther below the poverty line and resorted to ransacking bins to eke out a living.

"As things now stand, even good access roads into our community are dreams that may never be realised in our lifetime," said Mr Jeremy, a leading citizen of Niogo.

Mayor Dan Dakota and his men awarded endless contracts to political members and friends without checking if they were qualified and competent to execute such projects. They only thought of their ten per cent kickback or settlement, which was often paid directly into their foreign bank accounts as soon as the contract was signed. It was a common sight to see countless abandoned projects scattered far and wide, which had already been funded to the last cent.

The rat families in Mr O'Brien's bakery were well informed as to how Mayor Dakota ran his government, thanks to the smart spy mice who left no stone unturned to take the latest news to Mr Rodent and the Bakery Rat Community. Little did they know that there were surprises lurking in the corners of the bakery.

Now that success was beginning to knock on Mr O'Brien's door he was thinking of moving to larger premises in a better environment in the centre of the City of Canterborne as was befitting his new status. He would expand the bakery, thus providing additional room for his business and staff, and he would have a closer grip on his secret political ambitions. He worked even harder to realise this dream.

Mayor Dakota was not ignorant of the steaming political rivalry between himself and Mr O'Brien, and other pockets of political opponents here and there. Even when he had won the mayoral election putting him in power, the bitter rivalry only subsided a little, but he knew that it would hot up again sooner or later. Dakota was not the sort to back down regarding politics, and Mr O'Brien was in no doubt as to the bad luck the future held for him in the hands of a political enemy like the mayor. He knew it would soon come to a head, but he could not predict the way and manner in which Dakota would exploit his resources to avenge himself like a sniper's bullet.

A few months later, Mr O'Brien was in a coffee shop having a black coffee when he suddenly lurched forwards from his revolving chair, staring at a caption from the newspaper held by a fellow customer. He read, TOTAL BAN ON IMPORTATION OF WHEAT, CEREALS, FLOUR, SUGAR AND BUTTER, and it ended up with the final straw, BRACE UP FOR HOME-GROWN PRODUCTS OR STARVE...

Mr O'Brien could not wait long enough to finish his cup of coffee, but stormed out of the shop and dashed across the street to purchase a similar vanguard newspaper for an interrupted 'read and digest', as he would often say.

"I knew this bastard would fight back," he thundered to a friend who happened to be passing by. "This will send us back to the bread making era of the Stone Age. Home-grown produce is largely substandard and not found in great quantities, so we mostly rely on imported goods to cover the deficit. This action automatically translates to poverty and starvation for many, and it will spell doom for a young growing industry like ours," he said, pouring over the newspaper.

To Mr O'Brien it was a deliberate act of revenge on the part of Mayor Dakota and his men because it should have been a gradual measure to be introduced and spread over a long period of time to enable easy adaptation and less pain for the citizens of Canterborne. Those worst hit were the rats of the Bakery Rat Community in Mr O'Brien's shop. Initially, staple food rations came in smaller bags then trickles, and at one stage there were no leftovers to scavenge with only just enough food and cereal bags for the daily bread production. The staff took no chances with the meagre stocks in the storeroom, which were kept under lock and key. This made it extremely difficult for the rats to gain entry, and rat traps were strategically set to the detriment of those careless enough to toy with them.

Every rat was beginning to starve and some had to journey all the way to the jungle to find a daily meal. The jungle rats were already laying down rules on how to check the undue influx from the Bakery Rat Community, fearing the same fate might befall them even in the jungle. They were not just going to allow the migrant rats to invade their territory.

"All rats must carry their own burden," said Mr Konky, the jungle rats' mercenary leader.

Mayor Dakota's loyalists were thriving in a special way; the way of double standards. The so-called ban on cereals and the crazy home-grown stuff of his administration were for political rivals and enemies, not the chosen few. Anyone in the mayor's camp only needed a signature from him to automatically qualify to import anything they desired.

"Every political enemy is nothing but a mortal enemy and should be dealt with decisively," reasoned the mayor.

Some human and rat citizens of Canterborne could not wait to boot Dan Dakota out of office at the next election, and even some loyalists were beginning to have mixed feelings and resentment towards him. There were secret meetings afoot, and some of the mayor's dubious orders were subtly disobeyed. They could no longer close their eyes to the terrible events of the leadership of the day.

The educational sector of the city had been one of the worst to be hit, school leavers and graduates being a common sight roaming the streets in their thousands searching for non-existent jobs. It was almost unheard of to secure a position unless a godfather was powerfully linked to those at the helm of the city's affairs. It made no difference what grades were achieved, as merit was already out of the window. One had to be highly connected to make ends meet, or become a criminal to survive.

As a result of the situation, some smart young school leavers resorted to sharp practices and dubious activities such as drug peddling, oil bunkering, obtaining things under false pretences, robbery, pimping and prostitution, pickpocketing, counterfeit racketeering, money laundering and human trafficking.

"We can't find a decent job," was the only excuse offered when the perpetrators were caught – as if that justified their crimes.

Mr Justin Walkman left university with a first-class degree in languages and business administration, but was unable to secure an acceptable post after several years of job hunting. He finally decided to join forces with a few out-of work friends to register a business they named, 'Guess What International Ltd'. The aims and objectives of this registered business were not immediately known, for the friends dabbled in anything imaginable. Decency and reason were often thrown overboard and the only driving force was to make money and more money by whatever means possible to the detriment of those who were ripped off or hurt.

The business went underground scouting for profiles, names and addresses of successful individuals, businesses and companies, home based and foreign, to ascertain the nature of their business. After a detailed study, well-written, patronising business letters were mailed to each target, often composed by Justin Walkman because of his academic ability. The partners were then prepared to wait some time, with occasional prompting, to receive a reply.

Justin and his partners made sure they used the forged business letterheads of the City of Canterbourne's major oil refineries, duly signed and with more bogus claims as bait for their intended associates. They made sure that any money received went straight into their chosen bank accounts for easy withdrawal and laundering if necessary, nevertheless, payment was often requested in advance before delivery.

Hackman Ltd, a very successful, foreign offshore company, was among those promised a huge supply of crude oil at an extremely tempting low price, which beat any quotation they had ever received in the history of the company. They could not believe their luck.

"How can an obscure company in an oil rich nation have such easy access to supply crude oil of such a high quality and in this quantity, but at such a fantastically low price? We have struck gold," thundered Jerry Biancon, one of Hackman's top directors. "We have to act now before they change their minds," he reasoned.

Hackman Ltd paid two million dollars in advance, and the directors waited for the fictitious supply of oil that never arrived.

That was the first breakthrough from poverty for Mr Justin Walkman and partners of Guess What International Ltd. They quickly shared their loot, with Justin receiving one third of the proceeds as the idea had been his brainchild. What had begun as a game had now been transformed into a huge money-spinner and everyone was overjoyed.

"We must keep a low profile and play it close to our chests so that we do not arouse suspicion. We certainly cannot afford any exposure at present," warned Mr Justin Walkman.

Business was good except when the company occasionally received similar letters from rival companies offering dodgy deals. Such communications were gathered up and passed through the shredding machine into oblivion.

"You cannot rob Peter to pay Paul," Justin would say with an evil smile, intimating that he was not a man to be crossed over the lucrative shady deals.

A time came when Walkman and his partners, wanting to branch out, decided to invest in the property market.

"Houses never lose value," Justin boasted to his partners during his lecture on property development.

His friends looked upon him as a master of the game

whose advice, brainpower and guidance had turned them into millionaires over night. None of them was prepared to take his ideas for granted, especially in the present lucrative climate, and his challenging, infectious zeal and oratory had rubbed off on them.

"No one will be stupid enough to miss out on this new venture," said Mr Sam Piccolo, Justin's deputy director.

The property business began on an honest footing, but it soon became painfully obvious that not enough money could be made so, before they realised it, greed had taken over. They sold the same plot of land to three or four buyers using falsified documents, and were soon being summoned to appear in court so many times they lost count. This did not deter them, for they knew they had sufficient funds to bribe corrupt police officers and magistrates, and get away with it. Whenever their bubble burst and they were arrested, they bribed every government official involved in the case to throw it out of court through lack of evidence and witnesses. The swindlers' wealth gave them the freedom to continue their nefarious activities.

Once in a while the company came across a difficult client and often a compromise was reached whereby they were persuaded to accept half of the full payment for the property they purchased instead of losing everything and having to contend with the threat of possible murder on their mind. Justin and his partners had a dubious reputation, so citizens often chose the lesser evil and were happy to take half the money they had paid for the land, in the knowledge that they had escaped with their life.

As time passed, Justin and his partners fast became too notorious and greedy for their own good. Hundreds of acres with properties on them were sold to five different families in the same questionable way, but then the bubble burst. One buyer happened to be one of Mayor Dan Dakota's cronies, a Mr Colin Koka, the money used for the purchase being part of the City of Canterborne's treasury.

Mr Koka fronted for the mayor, a perfect cover, to negotiate deals whilst he sat on the sidelines and did not become involved for fear of citizens' wagging tongues. Now that the deal had turned sour, Dakota was ready for his pound of flesh from the criminals and pulled strings to regain his money, the property or both.

This quest left many victims in its wake. Mr Justin Walkman and his partners could not stand the heat, storm and dust raised by Mayor Dan Dakota and his loyalists, ranging from the state police department to the courtrooms. At the end of the day, no amount of bribery money could save them, and that dodgy deal was the last they ever negotiated. The founders of Guess What International Ltd were incarcerated in the City of Canterborne's maximum security prison serving life sentences for countless allegations, charges and convictions. This opened a floodgate of other investigations and reports on previous deals of extortion, fraud and obtaining under false pretences. The mayor managed to sort out life sentences for them instead of making them face a firing squad, as should have been the case if they had followed to the letter the constitution of the City of Canterborne for offences of such a magnitude. The mayor received his money and the controversial property in exchange for the usual death penalty that the criminals would have attracted.

At Mr O'Brien's bakery, the embargo had not been lifted on the importation of staple food materials and ingredients for bread production. The baker was still struggling to pay his staff and keep the business running. He had to cut corners by paying some of his closest friends, who were loyal to Dan Dakota's political party and had the right to import goods. He had to give them a percentage of the profits, but managed to coast along, sustaining his workers and the business. Luckily business was good, so he only had to top up the profits to break even.

The Bakery Rat Community was beginning to enjoy life

once again as things were falling into place, they were getting enough to eat and never forgot their task of reproduction. They made sure that a new baby was born every day by whatever means.

"There is sense in numbers," Mr Rodent would say.

He seriously encouraged the reproduction process, and the rat population had quadrupled, which made him happy.

"Soon the day will come when no corrupt leader will dare to mess with the rat community," he said.

One cold morning, Mayor Dan Dakota was having his breakfast of bran flakes and fruit with a hot, steaming cup of coffee, all set out on the dining table close to the lounge, his usual routine. He was in a good mood as everything seemed to be going his way. The delivery of the morning newspapers was important because very often the news made or marred his day. As he held one of the newspapers in his left hand, trying to scan the news headlines, he realised that there was no major negative news about his administration, except for a few lines about the arson of the treasury building headquarters. That was old news about his political detractors who were still clawing at whatever strategy they could to ruin his political chances.

Come next election, he told himself, I will have to do something about it like paying some leading journalists to write positive articles about my few political projects. I will manipulate the national news media to my own advantage. He decided he would have to talk to his communication secretary, Mr Parroty, before things got out of hand.

"Life is not worth living without political power," he often said to his cabinet members.

The mayor beckoned to one of his official bodyguards and asked him to contact Mr Parroty on his mobile phone and summon him to an immediate meeting to receive instructions. He did not want to risk discussing anything with him over the phone, for he could not afford to take any chances at that critical stage, not when his numerous political opponents were eager to pin things on him and pull him down by whatever means they had on their evil agenda. I will not let them and I must be one step ahead at all times, he thought.

He was still eating and thinking when Mr Mighty, one of Mr Rodent's spy mice stationed in the mayor's lounge, noticed some fallen crumbs under Dan Dakota's breakfast table. The empty feeling in his tummy was so bad that he dashed out into the open without thinking, making a beeline for the fallen bran flakes, all sense of reason and caution thrown to the wind as he allowed greed and hunger to take over. He was already out in the open when he remembered his mission, but he had been sighted by the mayor who immediately ordered his guard to chase and destroy the intruder. That was promptly executed, so with no escape route and all the fire doors locked, Mr Mighty became another casualty of the Bakery Rat Community.

After several weeks of receiving no news from Mr Mighty and not seeing him anywhere, Mr Rodent assumed he might have met his death, but he had to wait another six months to mourn his demise and send in another well-trained replacement, Mr Jingo Abel. This time gap was a foolproof way of convincing Mayor Dakota that there were no more mice living under his roof, so he relaxed and let slip his guard. Once again he became more open about his future plans as regards the running of the City of Canterborne and, above all, his political plans for the upcoming election.

The Bakery Rat Community mourned the demise of Mr Mighty, a blessed memory and one of their fallen heroes, for two weeks even though his body was never recovered. Despite this, .no one was deterred from the original plans of rat liberation, and the beat went on and on.

"Failure to keep track of Mayor Dakota's plans could be

likened to the stupid actions of a blind man in a dark room looking for a black shoe that is not even there," reasoned Mr Rodent. "Dakota is a man to be watched day and night, and too dangerous to be left alone. Our community cannot afford to slacken in their efforts to watch his every move and listen to his preconceived plans for the humans and rats of the City of Canterborne," he added.

# CHAPTER FIVE

MAYOR DAN Dakota left no stone unturned. Using a mystery middleman to launder his money, he ensured that much of the national treasury funds were stashed away into his personal foreign bank accounts, especially in Switzerland, with coded numbers that would be difficult to trace. In case he lost the election he wanted to be sure of hanging on to such ill-gotten gains without raising suspicious eyebrows.

He often despatched his men to dig out the dirt on his major political opponents to destroy their credibility. He wanted their past mishaps to be in the public spotlight to score cheap political points. His instructions were that even if no incriminating evidence was unearthed some should be created.

"Politics is a dirty game, we all know that," he often said to his numerous loyalists; hangers-on to the powerful for gain and favour falling from the master's table.

In the last few days running up to the election many were playing it safe, showing smiling obsequious faces, but no one knew what was really on their mind. Most knew that their mayor was ruthless and untrustworthy, so as election day drew close, every human and rat citizen of the City of Canterborne kept their fingers crossed. What could happen on D-Day was anyone's guess, as Mayor

Dakota could be as unpredictable as the weather most of the time. He was constantly spoiling citizens with unsolicited charity to win them over to his side for the forthcoming battle.

Every discovery of a new oil well in the City of Canterborne was automatically seen as additional personal wealth for Mayor Dan Dakota, who promptly sent his men to cordon off the area and quieten any community agitation that usually surrounded such an important incident. In the heat of the moment, local agitators, leaders who were the true voice of the people, would gather together for autonomy and self-determination, but were promptly arrested, detained and tried in one of the numerous emergency kangaroo courts. These so-called courts were presided over by magistrates or judges who had to conform to the wishes of the political leaders, carry out their dirty deeds or face their wrath. The agitators were eventually sent to jail for life or faced death by hanging.

The many who agreed with the agitators and hoped for resource control, were frightened at this outcome, so such protests fizzled out. The younger protesters went underground as guerrilla warlords, and continued their fight from there. They knew how Mayor Dan Dakota operated and they believed his fingers to be in every dubious pie in the City of Canterborne.

One bright December morning as the sun rose from the east to usher in the glory of the coming Christmas and citizens turned on their transistor radios to enjoy the usual seasonal melodies, out of the blue there was a sudden change of song.

"My fellow countrymen," Mayor Dakota's voice rang out, "there was a coup late last night by some disgruntled elements in the military, who banded together to overthrow my government. Luck was not on their side and they have been rounded up and overpowered by our loyal troops. They will face a military tribunal and if found guilty will be decisively dealt with in accordance with the military rules of the land. Thank you very much!"

A stunned silence greeted this ominous announcement. The few who knew Mayor Dan Dakota well enough understood the writing on the wall; this was one of the ways of destroying his perceived or imagined enemies on trumped up charges. He wished to be assured of winning the forthcoming election with few or no serious contenders. Those whose candidacy could barely win elections in their own constituency, let alone speak of winning major elections in the entire City of Canterborne, would be given a chance, but would be embarrassed.

As luck would have it, Mr Kalio O'Brien, the owner of the bakery that was home to several thousands of Bakery Rat Community families lead by Mr Rodent, was not included on the list of those charged with the treasonable offence. His political ability had not attracted the attention of Mayor Dakota's men, for he was thought of as a baby politician who should be left alone to wallow in his political mediocrity.

A few weeks later the national news media broadcasted that those arrested had been found guilty of a treasonable felony, and they were promptly executed by firing squad without having the chance to say a final goodbye to their families. Some who were desperate managed to pass on a message to their loved ones by sending wristwatches and other trinkets as memorabilia for their bereaved families.

Mr O'Brien thanked his lucky stars for this mysterious escape. He lay low and waited for the election process to begin. He seemed to have more supporters by the day and his list was secretly growing. Some of Mayor Dakota's loyalists came to the conclusion that he was too crafty to be trusted, so were double-dealing, and gradually pitching their political tents in Mr O'Brien's camp.

"It doesn't matter how loyal you are to him, he never trusts you and will often send others to closely monitor your activities and report back to him without your knowledge," said Mr Gabriel Jakarta, one of the mayor's numerous bodyguards.

Mr O'Brien continued to work hard in his bread making business, which was a perfect cover for him to groom his political ideas and secretly increase his number of supporters. Mayor Dakota thought of him as a dedicated baker, a small time businessman who had more important things to worry about like the importation embargo than politics.

Those citizens of the City of Canterborne worst hit by the embargo seemed to be the rats living in the Storage Rat Commuunity, for they barely had enough to eat in the midst of plenty. Even their mates in the Jungle Rat Community seemed to be better off because life for them was a game of the survival of the fittest; you either sank or swam with so much to worry about, including predators.

"How can one live by the river banks and yet wash hands with murky waters and mud? This is the true home of most of the nation's resources, yet we are left to feed on crumbs while the non-deservers eat meat and feed like kings, worst still at our expense. We honestly deserve better than this," said Mr Saros Kent, the Storage Rat Community leader, tears running down his cheeks.

Mr Kent was a courageous and emotional leader who wanted to bring about the burial rites for Mayor Dan Dakota's leadership. He had already met with other rat community leaders scattered around the city and outskirts of Canterborne. Plans were underway, and fingers were crossed that what was to come was not discovered.

The human and rat citizens of the city were losing patience. Some of the young secretly made effigies of Mayor Dakota, which they doused with fuel and set ablaze in mockery of his corrupt and insensitive rule. This seemed to serve as healing and calming massage for their troubled souls and minds after witnessing the unbelievable suffering, death, looting and rape that had become commonplace in their beautiful and blessed Canterborne. The city's abundant human and natural resources were being squandered by Mayor Dan Dakota and his men for their selfish ends.

# CHAPTER SIX

I**T WAS** on a very early August morning when the innocuous sensitive flowers of the mimosa were just beginning to welcome the dawn of a new day by religiously opening their tiny, folded foliated leaves to embrace the morning sun as it ascended from the horizon that Stewrat set out on an unusual adventure.

He was a young, curious and energetic member of the Bakery Rat Community whose life had been punctuated by his unquenchable thirst for adventure and taking silly risks. He was one of the rats who had narrowly escaped death by a whisker when he joined Mr Nutty's band on a surprising quest to visit the city centre in broad daylight in defiance of humans and to mingle with them. They wanted to discover if they would be welcomed as equals, but it was not to be. They were almost run over by a careless taxi driver, and posh children returning home from school pelted them with stones. They were lucky to have escaped with their lives by squeezing through a broken drainage cover, the drain being empty at the time or maybe they would have drowned and not lived to tell the tale to those of the rat community who cared to listen to their crazy adventure stories.

"Our lives were almost cut short by the terrible humans' iron house on four wheels that dangerously zoomed past us without a care in the world, fumes endlessly rushing from its bottom enough to make one sick as hell!" observed Stewrat, clearly referring to the taxi.

Beka, Stewrat's mother, had tried everything in the book to curb her son's insatiable appetite for fun, action and adventure. He had been out very early in the morning, hanging out with the wrong mates, and soon he was off to the jungle to visit some old friends. On his way he met a wandering young wildcat who had been left home alone whilst his mother, Kitty, dashed into the jungle in search of food for her young family. His father had left home, finding it convenient to get his wife pregnant then abandon the family rather than care for them. He claimed that the role of fatherhood was too demanding, one for which he was not cut out, so had fled from his responsibilities.

When young Stewrat met Lemo, the home alone wildcat, on the jungle path there was an instant mutual attraction and they immediately became friends. They were soon looking out for things with which to play, started to play hide-and-seek and then moved on to football, using small grains of corn Stewrat had stuffed into his mouth when raiding a farm on the way to the jungle. There was no goalpost, so they contented themselves with using whatever skills they had and running around. It was getting dusk and the friends were both tired, so Lemo decided to take Stewrat home to show him where he lived so that he could call again. His mother was not back yet.

"She's probably still scavenging for us," was Lemo's excuse for his mother.

"Never mind, most mothers are like that, mine too," replied Stewrat.

Lemo escorted his new friend halfway home. They hugged and promised to keep in touch then said goodbye and agreed to meet at the same time the following day with some toys with which to play.

Waiting at home, Stewrat's mother had been worried

sick as to his whereabouts and, fearing the worst, hoped he had not been killed by a cruel predator or had an accident. When he arrived home she was over the moon and was soon bombarding him with questions.

"Where have you been?"

"I met a new friend today. His name is Lemo and he is so nice," her son replied.

"Where does he live?" his mother enquired, wanting to make sure her son was keeping good company.

"He lives with his mother in the mountain caves in the remote part of the jungle. He is a member of the cat family – I mean small cats."

"What?" thundered Beka, raising one of her forelimbs. "You are never to see him again, do you understand?" she shouted.

"Why?" asked Stewrat.

"If you see him again run for your life and keep running, for they kill us for food, you could be their next meal. Run away as fast as your legs will carry you, OK?"

"Yes, Mum," Stewrat agreed, but he was still curious.

Back in the jungle, Kitty, Lemo's mother, had been searching everywhere for her son only to meet him on the pathway as he was returning home. She was so happy to see him.

"Where have you been?" she questioned.

"I've just seen a new friend off to his home," answered Lemo.

"Who is your wonderful new friend?"

"His name is Stewrat, a nice looking rat from the Bakery Rat Community."

"And you let him go?" cried Kitty, who had been wandering the jungle in search of food for her family.

My stupid son has let a good meal escape scot-free, Kitty thought.

"When you see him again, tear him to pieces and eat him, for he is your food."

Seeing how worried his mum was, Lemo said:

"All right, Mum."

A few days later, out of curiosity rather than reason, Stewrat went to the jungle once again in search of his new friend, Lemo. With his mother's warning ringing in his head like an alarm bell, he had to be more cautious.

Lemo was also looking for Stewrat, his new friend, also bearing in mind what his mother had told him. He was deep in thought when he suddenly looked up and saw him just a few metres away. They both stopped and gazed into each other's face trying to read their mind from facial expression. Stewrat noticed an unusual glint of fire in Lemo's eyes, mixed with unusually subdued excitement. Each pretended that all was well and expected the other to give the game away by inching closer or making a run for it. The tension was building up, so Stewrat, being very clever, decided to break the ice.

"Don't worry, Lemo, it's over, OK? Look for another meal. The story your mother told you was also told to me by my mother. We can't be friends for you are a predator, the killer of my race, so it's game over, bye, never to see you again."

Stewrat had said his bit then fled as fast as his feet could carry him until he was safely at home with Beka. He never told his mother where he had been even when his breathlessness almost gave him away. He was just grateful to be alive despite everything.

Mayor Dakota was so determined to win the coming election he hired the services of marabouts, sorcerers and fortune-tellers – even witch doctors.

"Your enemies will be your footstool," they often told him, convincing him more by displaying their magical powers in his presence.

These hirelings swept Mayor Dakota off his feet, for he truly believed in their world of magic. To him the entire world was nothing but a product of prestidigitation, probably designed by the greatest magician. These people were housed in one of the mayor's sprawling estates and they were supplied with every requested need, as long as they told him what he wanted to hear.

"How dare we tell him the whole truth and risk our lives and all these good things at our beck and call? Just study his mindset and tell him what he likes to hear, and that way you keep him in check and still have your good life," said Jakop, one of the marabouts, also revealing how a sorcerer was fired for telling the whole truth about things.

David Jones, one of the mayor's assistants, was entrusted with the duty of helping him to launder large sums of money into Swiss bank accounts. David diverted all the money into his own off-shore bank account in Bermuda and simply disappeared. He had double-crossed Dan Dakota, who secretly despatched his men to look for him.

David was a serious family man, who missed his two-year-old twin sons, five-year-old daughter, Tania, and his beautiful wife, Makozi. After ten months away, he was stupid enough to sneak back into the City of Canterborne in the middle of the night to secretly relocate his family to his new home in Toronto, Canada, where the long arms of the mayor would never reach him. He was spotted at Canterborne International Airport and gunned down by mayor Dakota's hooded killer in the presence of his family, just as they were about to board the next flight to Canada.

The media was quick to report that David's killer was part of a faceless, disgruntled drugs gang whom his victim seemed to have double-crossed, and that he was still at large. There were no witnesses, but the government was seriously trying to track down the criminal and would not rest until he had paid the price. Rumours went wild in the city, like a bush fire, and no one believed the news reports. Citizens were becoming suspicious of foul play every time a prominent member of society was eliminated under questionable circumstances. People seemed to guess what had happened, and they were often correct, but dared not speak out loud enough to point accusing fingers in the right direction, for fear of disappearing or suffering the same fate from the power brokers of the day.

Silent tension once again began to mount in the City of Canterborne and each time a situation arose, Mayor Dakota's only option was to take a long vacation to a luxurious Caribbean holiday resort. There he could escape incognito to squander his massive stockpile of the nation's wealth with beautiful ladies of easy virtue, often changing his name to avoid recognition and the problems associated media frenzy.

On one such vacation, the mayor met Nancia Abdul, a very attractive Caribbean lady with elegant legs and a taste for the good life, fashion and jewellery. She could be quite loud and assertive, and all eyes turned to adore her, something of which she was aware and used to her advantage. It was a cool evening when they met in the lounge of the Marriott Island Hotel where Dakota often stayed on his vacations. He was there under the false name of Dominic Patel, to avoid detection.

There were five groups of good looking young ladies sitting around the bar, having a laugh and sipping drinks. Among them was Nancia Abdul, who obviously stood out from the crowd. Dominic Patel was already swept off his feet by her beauty and he was leaving nothing to chance. He left his seat and walked towards Nancia, holding his glass of Bacardi and politely inching forwards.

"Hello, Princess. I'm Dominic Patel, do you mind if I buy you a drink?"

"Thank you," she replied as he gently lowered himself into the vacant seat beside her.

"What's your name please, if I may ask Your Majesty?"

"Call me Nancia, Nancia Abdul, if you like," she replied, beginning to acknowledge the important presence of Dominic, and being slightly carried away by the new way in which she had been greeted.

No man had ever addressed her in such a manner before and this Dominic just might be her Mr Right. You never know, she told herself thoughtfully.

Seeing that Nancia was giving this new man some attention, her friends made flimsy excuses and disappeared into the indoor swimming pool area of the large lounge, leaving their friend to her new man. The conversation and meeting were progressing well and one thing led to another. After several nights together, Dominic and Nancia soon became an item, but with so much money to spend they had to move to another hotel for fear of exposure and mostly for security reasons.

Mayor Dan Dakota was regularly in touch with the situation in Canterborne, his men furnishing him with daily reports. The news became better by the day and it was soon time to return home as tempers and tension had cooled with no more fear of reprisals. He suddenly decided to go back, furtively landing at a private airfield in a specially chartered jet belonging to one of his loyal men, Barry Clifford, an international businessman of dubious reputation.

Some weeks later, Mayor Dan Dakota announced that there were insufficient funds in the national treasury and the only way to rectify the financial mess was to take a bank loan of several million dollars. The exact amount was kept secret from the general public for reasons of accountability. The mayor said future generations would have to pay it back in the long term.

"This is a satanic alternative," said Mayor Dakota. "We either sink or swim as a nation, for without this loan our present situation is doomed. Every section of this government stands no chance, especially the health sector where the Aids pandemic is destroying every household in the

City of Canterborne and its fringes. I leave this decision as to whether to take the loan or not, as a national debate for everyone, and we shall cast our votes in a few months' time, the majority winning. I hope this is a well thought out issue and a fair democratic gesture by our noble government."

The mass media and rat and human citizens of Canterborne went into a frenzy, everyone being happy and satisfied that this kind of democracy stood as a good change of heart and a show of better understanding and maturity of a listening government, but a few days later...

"We are deeply sorry that just yesterday we obtained the bank loan. It is unfortunate we could not wait long enough for your deliberations and votes, nevertheless, we are marching on and shall triumph in unity. Thank you very much."

That was it. The curtain was drawn, that was the end of Mayor Dan Dakota's speech then other programmes came on the screen.

"That was it – another broken promise," thundered Mr Rodent.

It was rumoured that the mayor's secretary and political adviser, Mr Magade Robot, insisted that all had been executed in the best interests of the populace of the rats and human citizens of the City of Canterborne.

Back in the Bakery Rat Community everyone was warming up to secretly canvass for votes for Mr Kalio O'Brien in the coming election - without his knowledge. They were all making plans for their families as well. An election victory for Mr O'Brien would be victory for all and an opportunity for a better life. However, Mr Rodent had mixed feelings on the matter, for he found it really difficult to trust humans.

"You can see their faces, but what goes on in those awful minds is hidden from view," he said.

He felt that supporting Mr O'Brien was far better than joining Mayor Dakota's ranks. Everyone knew him for what he was and would stop at nothing to get him out of office. They were well aware of the power of their small stature, making it easy to sneak in and out of places even the ballot boxes if need be, but they hoped it would never come to that.

Kito Nino, one of the leaders of the Storage Rat Community scattered in the south of the city, also supported Mr O'Brien and often barred the young rats from even mentioning the name 'Dakota'. To him, the mayor was nothing but a nation looter.

"Fellow rats, he has robbed us blind," he often said if he heard the name mentioned by stubborn, young tearaway rats who loved to disobey the old school and taunted their leader for being old-fashioned.

Kito was known for his tough stand on matters about what he believed strongly, so it was no surprise when he bluntly refused to share his little room with his cousin who hoped to be offered a night's sleep. He was travelling on a special mission and couldn't afford to book into a hotel because of the high cost of accommodation in the oil-rich Storage Rat Community region. Kito feared for his life, claiming his cousin was endowed with a huge nose and wide nostrils.

"I can't sleep in the same room with him because I don't want to die of suffocation in my sleep. He could suck up all the air in the room like a vacuum cleaner and leave me struggling for a breath of fresh air. I think he is better off sleeping in my lounge – that I won't mind," he told a friend.

Mayor Dan Dakota had gradually fallen in love with Nancia Abdul, and he was often heard engaging in long distance telephone conversations with her. As their romance blossomed, Nancia simply relocated to the City Of Canterborne to live with the mayor, who was still an eligible bachelor. He had no alternative but to tell her the truth about his concealed identity and the fact that he was the incumbent mayor of Canterborne. Before the year had ended they were engaged and then married.

The wedding was top class, teeming with notable dignitaries and high powered politicians. It was reported that on their wedding day, after the marriage vows of 'for better, for worse', the Rev John Brown, guests and visitors were ushered to the reception hall with the large dance floor where everyone was expected to dance and make merry. There was much entertainment, assorted drinks and choice meals for all. While Dakota was busy outside chatting with an old friend, Nancia was equally busy on the dance floor chatting with her friends and telling them that her marriage to the mayor was simply:

"For better, mine darling; for worse, I've gone for good and I'm not coming back."

Everyone burst out laughing, thinking it was just a joke gone too far or maybe a product of alcohol, since everybody seemed to have had so much to drink. Little did they know that she meant every word, but how she intended to prove it in the midst of so much wealth cushioning their marriage was anybody's guess.

Nancia ensured that she had regular prompt deliveries of top-of-the-range latest fashions by great designers in clothes, jewellery and shoes. She told her friends that money for her was no problem, the only problem being how to spend it. They all envied her new status.

The financial adventures and corrupt practices of Mayor Dakota and his cronies as they fleeced what remained of the City of Canterborne's national treasury were not in question. As a result, other sectors of the economy were left to suffer greatly or overlooked entirely and abandoned, especially health, education and the general welfare of the citizens. Hundreds of thousands of rat and human families were living in squalor and scavenging from the streets.

Mr Norbat Dikom, one of the mayor's cabinet ministers, was interviewed on a live television show by foreign journalists who wanted to uncover the truth about the state of the nation.

"I can't believe that the majority of our people are that poor, as I've yet to see anyone feeding from a dustbin," he thundered.

It was a common sight to see children dropping out of school whilst others struggled to complete their education. Even if they did finish school, they could not secure a job to compensate for all their hard work. Many were even worse off on a community sponsored programme, unable to bring glory to the populace who had suffered so much to educate them. Out of defiance, some became entangled in vices such as prostitution, pickpocketing, mugging and, at times, bare-faced robbery.

Dr Pete O'Kabuka, the shadow health secretary, was a dedicated and highly respected physician. He happened to be one of the few lucky ones to have studied medicine at the Royal College of Medicine in the UK on a community Christian Missionary Scholarship, his reward for being a steadfast young convert to the mission in those days. He had spent time working in various hospitals and with medical professionals in the UK and USA, and had decided to return home to help the people of the City of Canterborne. He had been honoured with his position by Mayor Dan Dakota, however, he had to liaise with Mr James Bolezi, the mayor's personal advisor on health matters and a man of little education. Mr Bolezi saw Dr O'Kabuka as a constant threat to his elevated cabinet position.

"He is too well educated and could one day take over my job and force me into joblessness and the teeming labour market. I honestly fear for my future and my position," Mr Bolezi confided to Mr Joe Obika, a close friend.

Dr Pete O'Kabuka had been working on an Aids programme, collecting data on the recent increase of HIV/AIDS and other ailments in the city. It seemed to him that the government was doing too little to combat the Aids virus, which was spreading and fast becoming a pandemic affecting almost one family in every five. People were not having safe sexual relationships and those who had become prostitutes as a result of poverty were compounding the problem, the younger generation being hit the hardest. The speed with which the virus was spreading was not abating when Dr Pete O'Kabuka made his findings available to Mr James Bolezi for onward submission to Mayor Dakota.

Six months later, nothing seemed to have been done to encourage Dr O'Kabuka. There were no contingency plans backed up with funds on how to battle the raging Aids pandemic, which was now ravaging families – babies, the young and elderly – and no one in the City of Canterborne was spared the agony.

Mayor Dan Dakota and Mr James Bolezi were more interested in stashing money away in foreign bank accounts in preparation for the forthcoming election. Grants from various charities and other international organisations to help with healthcare for Aids sufferers were often diverted with impunity. The apparent carefree attitude towards the general health and well-being of the citizens did not go down well with the professional and ethical beliefs of Dr O'Kabuka, who later learned that his submitted earlier research data had been thrown in the bin.

"Too academic, self-seeking and above all unduly patronising," were the very words used by Mr James Bolezi as he struggled to convince the mayor to look the other way and concentrate on winning the election rather than wasting time on a stupid incurable disease.

Dr Pete O'Kabuka was perturbed by these actions and vowed that he would prove his point, the reason why he had left the good life in the civilised western world on a 'rescue mission' of his own. He intended to shame the mayor and his many cronies, who often gave Dan Dakota bad advice to satisfy their own selfish needs. The doctor liaised with reliable foreign HIV/AIDS charities that were totally committed to furnishing him with the retroviral drugs needed to stem the outbreak. All this would have been more successful had the government become more involved in the campaign instead of turning a blind eye as they continued to further their political ambition.

Andre Kaku, a father of seven, was infected by his wife who had recently died of Aids leaving him with the children, six of whom had also contracted the virus. Akitu, the youngest eight-year-old son, had tested negative for the deadly disease, but had to drop out of school to tend to the bedridden members of the family. He was often seen shuffling from house to house in the rich neighbourhood in search of menial jobs like washing and ironing, cooking, running errands, fetching water and cleaning. He did endless household chores for the wealthy to eke out a living to support his dying family. They could barely stand much less do anything for themselves, the fabric of human strength having been eaten up by the fatal virus.

Young Akitu was often underpaid by his various masters because he was not attached to a registered agency, but he never complained because he loved his family and wanted to see them recover, not believing in the terminal nature of the illness.

"Don't worry, one day you will all get better," Akitu said, trying to encourage them whilst struggling to pay for their daily medication and care.

Sometimes Akitu entered the jungle to gather firewood to sell for additional funds, and on some occasions he was invited to Cayon village, far from Canterborne, to do menial jobs.

"My child has now become the father," his father mur-

mured from his death bed.

Andre Kuku appreciated his poor son's struggle and battle to save their lives from the virus that was determined to drag them down to the land of no return. The entire family now depended on the eight-year-old boy for everything, and the huge burden was proving too heavy for his young shoulders to carry. He had completely forgotten about his personal needs and well-being, so looked dirty, haggard and frail, all his energy and resources ebbing away. Passers-by often saw him crying bitterly and biting his lips as he wondered what wicked burden nature had placed upon his young shoulders with no adult help. He was saddened when he came across his former schoolmates each morning as they passed by on their way to school - he was on his way to knock on the doors of the wealthy to beg for menial jobs.

Adrian Melua of Bubbles Bubbles palm wine parlour was very popular in Cayon village. He was the village palm wine tapper, and everyone in Cayon and from afar travelled long distances to patronise his fashionable establishment. To most it was a fun haven; a place to sit and drink then forget all worries and spiritually disappear into the new euphoric world, a temporary distant refuge from the grim reality of the socio-economic and political mess of Mayor Dan Dakota and his cronies' chaotic regime.

In this way, Adrian Melua had saved many from the clutches of insanity caused by the wicked political leadership of the day. His numerous customers loved what he offered. Those men who found it hard to muster an erection for their wives requested the sediment from the bottom of the keg, as this was said to produce the required result. This was quite expensive, nevertheless, those in need were prepared to foot the bill.

Bubbles Bubbles provided a good excuse for antisocial behaviour at times including vices like drunkenness, drug abuse, rape, robbery and prostitution. Adrian Melua was nicknamed 'Bubbles Bubbles'.

"Who cares about his real name as long as he provides good palm wine, that's all that really matters," claimed Joshua, a wine parlour regular.

Adrian had started in the trade as a lad of seven with his father, Joe Melua, having refused formal education because of the corporal punishment administered by some teachers. He promised his father he would be good and do well in the palm wine-tapping business. Joe saw no reason why he should not encourage his son to carry on his trade, and quietly agreed with Adrian's decision. He taught him the tricks of the trade and helped his son to establish his feet firmly in the business.

When his father died, Adrian inherited the family business, became his own boss and decided to rename it Bubbles Bubbles, his own nickname and a clear reference to the way his wine bubbled from the local calabash cups and at times a hollow cow-horns from the local abattoir in Cayon.

# CHAPTER SEVEN

AKITU KUKU'S financial commitment to his bed-ridden family was beginning to take its toll on him now that he had taken another menial job in Cayon village and had to travel about 20 miles from Canterborne. His father and siblings were deteriorating fast due to insufficient funds to purchase the required drugs to slow down the pace of the virus.

Sometimes Akitu substituted their medication with that of cheaper and inferior quality, unfortunately all that he could afford. He resorted to the services of a bogus local herbalist who claimed to have the ability to cure all ailments with one single concoction. What else could he do? He had been abandoned by his extended family who turned a blind eye to his suffering even though many had benefited from the kindnesses and generosity of Andre Kuku in better times before he had spent his fortune on treatment and tests, only for the family to be diagnosed positive for the HIV/AIDS virus. There was no one to lend the family a helping hand for everyone seemed to have vanished into thin air, not wanting to offer support to their one-time benefactor, so it fell upon the only healthy son to work for a pittance with the last vestige of strength he had left.

This intolerable situation caused Akitu to jump at an offer by Lord Stephen Kobis, a retired politician and wealthy pig farm and racehorse owner. He dealt with bookies and racing dealers, and often travelled out of the country for business meetings and holidays. Michael, Joe and David Okon worked on his farm, but took liberties during Lord Kobis's long absences, neglecting their farm and ranch house duties, and spending most of their time in a drunken stupor at Bubbles Bubbles wine parlour.

Their luck ran out when Lord Kobis unexpectedly returned home from an overseas trip. On news of his arrival, the inebriated workers staggered back to the ranch from the wine parlour, forced open the storeroom, found the spades and frantically started to clear the rubbish that had accumulated in the house and pigsty. They sat on the grass to rest and instantly fell fast asleep, their spades beside them as they snored in deep slumber, the wine having got the better of them.

Lord Kobis was shocked by the mess in which he found his business and, on looking at the field, saw his dedicated staff asleep. He moved closer, only to discover that his employees' breath smelled of alcohol. He quickly typed out their letters of dismissal and put them in envelopes, which he stuck to their palms with Sellotape. When they eventually awoke they guessed what had happened and, knowing their employer to be a shrewd no-nonsense businessman, made their way off his land feeling very foolish and bowing their heads in shame.

Ralph, Lord Stephen Kobis's friend, introduced him to Akitu Kuku, who was given the job of sorting out the filthy pig farm and stables. He began working at weekends, but was soon asked to work all week, which meant more wages for the young lad, although he only visited his family at the weekend. He hoped to raise enough money for medication and food, as the meagre rations in the house had run out by the time the weekend came.

Akitu was paid 100 dollars a week for a job well done,

the most he had ever received. He took a shower and got dressed ready for his journey to Canterborne. He knew Cayon like the back of his hand having worked there before, and he certainly knew of Bubbles Bubbles wine parlour, which was located on the corner of the wide street adjacent to the home of Lord Stephen Kobis, from where he had just collected his pay packet. He was so happy to be heading home, knowing full well that he would put smiles on the faces of his dying family, especially his father.

He was fully aware of the long journey before him, having made it many times before. However, he decided to make the trek on foot, for he was determined not to spend a cent of his hard-earned wages on transport. He smiled to himself at the thought of how he would please his father and make him proud. Andre Kuku had often voiced his appreciation of his young son's care for the family and Akitu just wanted to see him smile, telling him there was hope in the midst of hopelessness.

Akitu's mind was so pre-occupied by those thoughts that he had lost all sense of time and darkness was falling fast. There were fewer travellers on the dirt path as he walked across the pedestrian walkway across the motorway. He occasionally passed others going in the opposite direction to Cayon or Obioma village, the home of great wrestlers and hunters. Some advised him to walk faster or find a place for the night, as it was too dangerous for a young boy to be out alone on the evil pathway after dark. He was told that men and boys under the influence of alcohol from Bubbles Bubbles often frequented the area in the hope of attacking vulnerable people.

"This pathway is not the best of places to be at this hour of night," he was told.

Akitu merely listened and nodded with a word of thanks for their concern, but continued on his journey. He negotiated a corner leading him to the next street, leaving the bushy pathways behind him and still having 15 miles to walk to Canterborne. Under a heavily-laden mango tree, just a few metres ahead, sat four, hooded, hefty-looking young male teenagers chatting amongst themselves as they smoked marijuana. Akitu could smell the pungent aroma from the drug, it was 9 pm and he wondered why they were not at home with their parents. He thought he should mind his own business as they were nothing to do with him, but when they saw him they became uneasy, moved closer to each other and communicated in low tones amongst themselves. That aroused his suspicions, but before he could turn around and make a run for it he heard:

"Stop there! Empty your lousy pockets and hand everything over."

The tallest of the gang had spoken.

"I've got nothing to hand over," replied Akitu.

Before he had finished speaking, the gang was upon him like flies, kicking and hitting him with the butts of their short guns. As this was done, one was busy checking out his pockets, turning them inside out and eventually making away with his hard-earned wages. The beating intensified until Akitu blacked out and, believing he was dead, the attackers started to run away.

"We can't just leave him there lying in the street. Passers-by will soon find his dead body, word will go around then the police will arrive. Come on, guys, let's drag his body to that abandoned warehouse so that by the time he's found he will have decomposed beyond recognition – that way we will at least be safe," said the leader of the hooded gang as they ran.

They all agreed that it was a good idea, so they retraced their steps and dragged Akitu's seemingly lifeless body into the warehouse, which was a few metres from the road and hidden in dense undergrowth. They then disappeared into thin air.

Akitu was bleeding profusely from his head, nose and

mouth, and with no help at hand was gradually slipping away into the world of the unknown…

The radiant sun shone down brightly on Cayon village, making everyone feel like playing and having fun.

Lord Stephen Kobis and his friends and guests were at Bubbles Bubbles wine parlour, sitting around a beautifully crafted bamboo table under a heavily-leafed mango tree, which served as an umbrella for the many customers. They were lazily drinking palm wine, chattering and joking. Richard Josty, Stephen's close friend, began to tell a story about a mystery man called Johnny who awoke early one morning to behold a stray foreign parrot perched comfortably on a flowering hedge in his beautifully kept garden. He quickly jumped out of bed, sneaked into the garden and crawled towards the unwary visitor as it busily pecked at insects and ants in the hedge. When close enough, the man jumped at the bird like a goalkeeper, clasping it with both hands as the terrified creature fluffed out its beautiful feathers, squawked loudly and became very agitated in its desperate attempt to escape.

"Where is your visa? Where are your immigration papers?" yelled Johnny. "Come on, shut your trap and here we go straight to the laboratory to check you out – for birds' flu."

By the time Richard had finished the tale everyone was roaring with laughter amid tears of joy. He saw that the keg of palm wine on the table was running low, so ordered a refill for his friends.

Akitu Kuku was miraculously discovered the next day in a hopeless state. Mr Pepper Temba, the City of Canterborne's food merchant, had gone to Cayon to inspect the abandoned warehouse with the view of purchasing it for renovation, for he was desperate to find additional storage for his new stock. As he was about to enter the building with the estate agent, they saw a terribly bruised, critically ill young boy lying on the grass.

They called the emergency ambulance, which arrived and took Akitu to Cayon Hospital's accident and emergency department for treatment.

The team of doctors who checked Akitu said his case was a sorry one and that he might not survive his injuries. He had sustained three broken ribs, a broken nose and a fractured skull.

"His survival will be a miracle," predicted Dr Pete O'Kabuka.

Their small patient had lost a lot of blood, and had Mr Pepper not chanced to find him he would certainly have died from such severe injuries. He was given several blood transfusions and adequate medical care in the hope that he would survive his ordeal. Medical services were not free in the City of Canterborne or Cayon village, so caring well-wishers raised the required amount of money. Dr Pete O'Kabuka made a generous donation and also donated his own blood, as his blood group matched that of Akitu. He was determined to get the boy to survive despite there only being a slim chance and the fact that they knew almost nothing about him except that he had probably been mugged in the notorious area in which he had been found. Nobody had come forward to identify the culprits.

Akitu was in a coma for four days and was fed through a tube inserted in his nostril. He had undergone a series of surgical operations for his broken bones, and he was now more stable, but still unconscious.

In the Bakery Rat Community, Mr Kalio O'Brien had provided rat families with shelter without permission. Although Mr Rodent did not have much faith in Mr O'Brien's political ability he was determined to drum up support for him as any alternative was better than Mayor Dan Dakota regaining office and continuing to snuff out the lives of the rat and human citizens of Canterborne. He sent Mr Nutty and some others to Cayon village to pass on the news of their political choice of Mr Kalio O'Brien, and to say that all residents should come en masse to cast their votes for him on election day. They had no money to splash out on bribes like Mayor Dakota and his cronies, who were giving free gifts of cars during the campaign, but the citizens of Canterborne did have principles, history, a conscience and determination to spur them onwards.

Mayor Dan Dakota doled out money to poor families at the slightest opportunity, believing implicitly in the power of money and politics.

"I'll scratch your back and you'll scratch mine, that is how it works," he was often heard to say to the electorate during the campaign, especially to those who had benefited from his overnight generosity.

The numerous spy mice despatched by Mr Rodent to various locations to report on Mayor Dakota's movements and plans were really doing a great espionage job. The latest news was about free handouts of money to media corporations in the City of Canterborne and the surrounding area, and how the mayor was telling people to discredit his opponent's manifesto as complete rubbish.

"Those empty promises show the desperation of a drowning man," Mayor Dakota told them. "There is sense in continuity," he assured them.

Whilst some accepted his bribes, but knew the truth, others allowed his propaganda to get into their heads and did his bidding. Mr Rodent scorned the mayor's continuity theory as the cry of a mad dog.

Akitu regained consciousness some weeks later and was discharged from the intensive care unit after further satisfactory tests and results. Dr O'Kabuka had been something of a patron to the boy, taking it upon himself to be his guardian because of his courage and survival against all medical odds. He had invested his own money to ensure that Akitu received the best treatment.

The young lad told the story of his family, and how he had been attacked and robbed by a hooded teenage gang of muggers when returning home after working hard for a week at Lord Stephen Kobis's estate. He had been in Cayon Hospital for two and a half weeks and all he could think of was his dying family back in Canterborne. He hoped that Dr O'Kabuka could help him to be reunited with them, which he promised to do, and would personally accompany him home to Canterborne by ambulance. He assured Akitu that he would do all in his power to make sure he received regular visits from his nurses to monitor his recovery.

Akitu, Dr Pete O'Kabuka and his medical team arrived by ambulance and entered the large bamboo fenced compound containing Akitu's home in the early hours of the morning just as the cock was crowing. A heavy silence greeted them, the place was deserted, and doors and windows were securely locked. The travellers alighted from the ambulance and looked around the empty compound. Akitu strolled over to the front door and knocked, but there was no response, so he knocked again – still no response.

"Let's break down the door," he said.

A single kick from Dr O'Kabuka made the door fly wide open and they entered the house, Akitu leading the way. There was an odd odour hanging in the air, and each room they accessed was neat and tidy with an empty bed. His father's bedroom and those of his siblings were all immaculate, but they noticed the gradual build-up of dust and cobwebs.

A multitude of thoughts were racing through Akitu's mind, spreading like wildfire.

"Let's contact the city police officers. They should have answers as to where Papa and the others are," he suggested.

As they entered the ambulance to leave, a uniformed policeman with a baton in one hand and a smouldering Benson and Hedges cigarette in the other indicated that they should stop as he walked towards them. He had been guarding the Kuku family home for a few days and had just returned from purchasing cigarettes from a nearby shop.

"Hi, I'm PC Damian. May I know what your mission is in the compound?" he asked. "I am on guard here."

"I am Dr Pete O'Kabuka, this is my medical team and this young man is Akitu Kuku. He is recovering from a serious mugging and has been in a coma in Cayon Hospital for a couple of weeks. When he regained consciousness he asked to be reunited with his family, and that is why we are here."

"Haven't you read the newspapers lately?" the policeman enquired.

"No, not at all. We are acutely short-staffed and have been extremely busy trying to save lives. On returning home, we are too exhausted to pick up a newspaper let alone read it, and even watching television is a problem. I simply don't have the time, so what's the news? Could you please tell us all you know as we are very anxious?" the doctor pleaded, as he watched Akitu's worried expression.

"It was exactly a week today when we received a mysterious phone call in the middle of the night, the solemn weak voice of a middle-aged man who seemed to be fighting his last battle with death. He simply said, 'Pl-e-a-se h-e-lp m-e,' and the phone went dead," the policeman related. "It took us several hours to trace the whereabouts of the strange caller and by the time we arrived he was already stone dead, his lifeless body lying at the foot of the bed. The terrible stench pervading the air in the Kuku home made us nauseous. We broke into the other rooms and were shocked to the core, for there were six decomposing corpses lying on beds. We decided the family had probably died in their sleep one after the other over a short period of time. We called the accident and emergency department at Canterborne Hospital, and the ambulance soon arrived and transported the corpses to the mortuary to await autopsy. How you people didn't hear the gruesome news beats me."

The policeman turned to young Atiku.

"It is a great shame, son. Please accept my sympathy," he said.

Akitu slumped to the floor in a dead faint, and was immediately rushed to Canterbourne Hospital where he was admitted to the emergency ward, with numerous police officers and reporters waiting in the wings to interview him on many issues when he recovered. They were all itching to hear the details, for due to many unforeseen circumstances his family had been cut off from the outside world until it had been too late.

Professor Tonga Briggs was the only consultant neurologist in the City of Canterborne and the surrounding area, so he often shuttled to and fro between the many clinics and hospitals within the region. He was to study Akitu's brain scan to give the go ahead on suitable medication and further treatment for the young patient, but the professor was nowhere to be found. He had not been seen for a few weeks. Patients on the critical list were being left to suffer in agony and some unlucky ones died before receiving help. Akitu's tests had been carried out and the consultant was now required more than ever, for he was needed to save the young lad's life.

After an exhaustive search with waiting lists for Professor Briggs growing daily a bombshell was dropped. The professor had left the City of Canterborne for pastures new; in the western world another case of brain drain on the already floundering health sector. A junior colleague said the consultant had been complaining of low wages and a heavy workload, but little did everyone realise that he would leave for good.

Akitu's condition became more critical as a search was

mounted to find another consultant to look at the boy's results. Dr Pete O'Kabuka, on hearing about the increasingly difficult situation, decided to see for himself. When he arrived from Cayon, Akitu had made no improvement, but he managed to open his mouth and speak with his last breath.

"Don't give up until you have found a cure for Aids..."

Akitu passed away clutching the doctor's hand. Dr Pete O'Kabuka closed Akitu's eyes sadly.

"Akitu didn't deserve to die like this," he protested. "The poor boy lost the will to live after losing his entire family, and the shock was too much for his already bruised, battered and painful body to bear. This is a great human tragedy."

He angrily turned to Dr Harry Akon, a close colleague who had accompanied him.

"It's high time Europe and the West stopped robbing us of our experts and professionals, leaving us with quacks and the untrained. They should find suitable staff elsewhere or start some sort of rota. What do you reckon, Harry?"

"Honestly, I would have thought that Europe and the West would have been more lenient after we laid the foundation of their nations' success on the slavery of our forefathers - their toil, pain, sweat and tears on those plantations. At least we deserve the justice of fair trade and possible reparation, not the brain drain of our few professionals. It's not too much to ask. I'm even afraid that one day we might all end up as prisoners going to our graves with the hope of millions of unfulfilled promises," reasoned Dr Akon.

The two colleagues were still deep in discussion when the deafening siren of the emergency ambulance was heard arriving with a new load of casualties.

Akitu was buried at Canterborne Church cemetery beside his father, mother and siblings, which closed the chapter on the once happy Kuku family. HIV/AIDS had finally won again as usual, leaving sorrow and tears in its wake.

# CHAPTER EIGHT

MR MAGADE Robot, Mayor Dan Dakota's political advisor, visited Paris in France and loved what he saw, wanting the same for the City of Canterborne.

One morning he awoke feeling disgusted about the poor state of the old buildings and shopping malls where the majority of rat and human citizens eked out a living. He demanded an emergency meeting with the mayor.

"Our city is extremely unsightly with all these ancient, dilapidated buildings and shops scattered everywhere," he pointed out. "Your Worship, it is time we did something about it, maybe demolish them and replace them with modern ones like I saw in Paris and other places in the Western world. I know our people will complain, but they can't keep that up forever can they? Once it's done, it's done."

The mayor listened attentively, for he believed in Mr Robot. He pondered over the issue for awhile.

"What's the alternative for my people and the rat citizens of the City of Canterborne?" he asked.

"They would have to wait for the new mansions and modern shopping complexes, but I promise it won't be too long a wait."

"Then you have my blessing, so go on, this might even

boost our success in the coming election as punishment for the stupid ones who have denied us votes in the past," emphasised the mayor.

Little did they know that every word of their dastardly plan was being noted by Mr Jingo Tega, a spy mouse, squatting comfortably beneath the mayor's sofa. As soon as it was midnight, the furtive spy sneaked out through the back and off to the Bakery Rat Community to report to Mr Rodent. He narrated the details of the plans afoot to destroy homes and shopping centres leaving the citizens of Canterborne with no alternative accommodation.

"These actions would be nothing but sheer wickedness. How can they destroy people's homes, shopping centres and livelihood with a vague promise of erecting modern buildings, which will never materialise? After all the looting of the national treasury this can only result in one thing; the citizens of the City of Canterborne would not only be fighting starvation, but also disease and a lack of family accommodation."

Mr Rodent turned and looked Jingo straight in the eye.

"Thank you very much, this is good news and we shall work on it. Now you can return to your post, and be careful not to be detected," he pleaded.

Some weeks later, many bulldozers were pulling down homes and shops without a care in the world. Everyone was wailing and crying in protest, but to no avail for the demolition was endless. Mr Magade Robot's men were having a laugh, a warning sign for those who might want to use their free will in the coming election.

Ever since the early days at the Bakery Rat Community, when Mr Nutty had seen Mr O'Brien helping Anita, his daughter, with her alphabet and numbers homework, he had longed to read and write like humans. He knew he was intelligent, but to master the human magic of the alphabet and 'numbers was altogether something else. He aspired to rise above his mates and, after much thought, came to the reasonable conclusion that the only way to achieve this was to learn the human's magic.

In the teeming, largely illiterate, population at the bakery, the ability to read and write, although not on the human scale, would rightly put him into the same league as Mr Rodent, Mrs Messy and a very few others who had wisely followed the same route in the early days of Anita's education. He chose to learn, so that he had the ability to read and write just a little, at the risk of his own life.

After school each evening, Mr O'Brien regularly helped his daughter with her lessons after she had eaten and rested. He had had little education and was determined his daughter would be well educated, even to the point of hiring home tutors when he no longer understood her homework.

Mr Nutty was aware of all this, and made sure he sneaked around eavesdropping and picking up pieces of the lessons while safely hidden well out of sight to avoid the danger of detection. He secretly visited the bakery bins to retrieve some of the disposed writing materials then spent the greater part of the night in his burrow teaching himself instead of going out hunting. He had to remember what Mr O'Brien had taught Anita, and very soon he was scratching out some letters of the alphabet and numbers. This was just enough to earn him respect among the rat families of his community.

Mr Nutty's first letter of the alphabet, 'A', was a sketch of a ladder with a single rung across it, the sides forced to meet at the top end, formed on the sandy floor of the bakery. He practised this repeatedly until he had mastered it then went on to the letter 'B'. This was two zeros or circles forced together standing on top of each other, with a final stroke drawn at the front joining the circles together firmly. His 'C' was a big circle with part of the front rubbed off. He did the same thing as he learned the numbers. This smart rat tried every trick in the book until he was able to reach a reasonable level of learning the 'human magic of the alphabet and numbers'. He took pride of place among his mates, who never ceased to admire his wisdom, courage and perseverance in 'going for it'.

"You are just like a common prisoner once your right is taken away from you," Mr Nutty would say, for he believed in freedom at all costs.

He could not understand why the Bakery Rat Community rats, himself included, could not walk the streets of the City of Canterborne in broad daylight with their heads held high without fear of molestation or even death.

He remembered one day that he would not forget in a hurry, a fateful day when he decided to try a visit to the city with five mates, one of whom was from the Jungle Rat Community. It was quite a long and tortuous journey, but they made it at last by brazenly crossing the human tar motorways. Their mission was to visit the great city to see what it actually looked like in bright sunshine during the daytime, and to feel the pulse of acceptability or rejection from those in power.

"Why should we always have to sneak about only at night and wait for darkness to fall before going out?" questioned Mr Totem, one of Mr Nutty's mates.

"It is now time to defy these inhuman rules and have our say," replied Mr Nutty.

When they reached the city centre and were standing by the road near the pavement, a large car swerved into the friends, almost knocking one of them over. They were lucky to have taken cover just in time to avoid a catastrophe. Before they could cross the road, they saw a group of posh looking school children pointing at them, running in their direction then pelting them with stones, a sign of deep-rooted hostility.

"Run for dear life! We are not welcome in their reserved areas," cried Mr Nutty, as they all took to their heels with the children in hot pursuit.

Luckily they escaped through an open manhole cover to safety. It had been a terrible experience for the young friends and they all vowed to work tirelessly to bridge the inequality, and even harder for their freedom.

On returning home they related their experience to Mr Rodent and others of the community who cared to listen.

"They have already passed on this terrible feeling to their children and now no one wants us near certain parts of our own city in the daytime. Can you believe this? We were almost run over by one of their iron houses on four wheels with noxious fumes that shoot out of its bottom and make one feel sick as it zooms past. I bet the driver must be wetting his pants by now hoping he has run over us at terrible speed as though he was in a competition for a trophy," Mr Nutty pointed out.

"Some of these cruel life experiences only succeed in moulding Mr Nutty's revolutionary and rebellious tendencies," said Mr Torki, a friend.

Even when Mr Nutty had been a young upstart in the Bakery Rat Community, Mr Rodent and the community had always believed in him, for they knew he could be counted upon in difficult times. Now all everyone could think about was to increase the rat population at all costs.

"There is wisdom in large numbers," emphasised Mr Rodent.

A few months later, Mr Nutty informed Mr Rodent that he had had a vision and would be glad to be given the opportunity to share it with the community.

"It came to me in the form of a poetic message written in the 'human's magic alphabet'. I was able to memorise it and I intend to share it with everyone in the Bakery Rat Community," said Mr Nutty.

Mr Rodent had a lot of respect for the young rat and immediately agreed to his request without any hassle.

"He is a good lad and I will bet my money on him any

time, any day."

Mr Loudmouth, Mr Rodent's personal secretary, was immediately summoned to disseminate the information of Mr Nutty's vision. A date was fixed for a meeting at midnight in the mixing and kneading room, when Mr O'Brien's staff were safely out of the way. The room had a raised platform that would serve as a podium.

When the day came, everyone was eager to find out what Mr Nutty had to say. The community respected him for his cleverness, bravery, comportment and intelligence, and they all wanted to find out the wisdom his oval head contained. He was summoned to come forwards and tell of his vision in the presence of the whole community, so he stood up and climbed to the top of the mixing and kneading table. He loved to show off his mastery of the human magic of the alphabet, and was always looking for another excuse to parade his expertise.

"You are welcomed to this great occasion," he began, after clearing his throat. "I feel greatly honoured by your presence and thank you all so much for attending." He paused to enjoy the applause that followed. "A few weeks ago, in my burrow, I went into a trance and things were revealed to me in a vision. I quickly memorised and wrote down the details in the hope of sharing it with everyone one day. I am happy that day has come."

Mr Nutty turned around and walked briskly to the other corner of the podium then revealed a medium-sized piece of white cardboard designed with a single sling by which it could be hung from the wall. He hung his chart on a lone nail in the wall behind him. On the chart the previous day he had carefully written words in the form of a poetic message. He volunteered to read and explain the words, and sing it later for their better understanding. He told them it would be their anthem, if Mr Rodent approved.

Rats of Third World
Rats of Canterborne

Rats of Jungle and Bakery,
Let's liberate ourselves from mankind;
Dodgy leaders of our land.
Day in, day out; empty promises
Lies upon lies every day,
Desperate attempts to run our lives
Shall be thwarted at all costs.
Sooner than later
Our trees of freedom
Shall grow like mustard seed.
We'll flourish and flourish
To the glory of rats' world.

By the time Mr Nutty had finished and later turned it into a song, everyone was eager to join him on the podium with much applause and wild shouts of boisterous excitement. Mr Rodent was the one who later discovered that the beautiful rendition of freedom was actually a piece of a sonnet. The entire rat community unanimously agreed to permanently adopt the sonnet as their anthem to urge them onwards for total freedom from the clutches of wicked and corrupt leaders like Mayor Dan Dakota in the City of Canterborne.

From that day it became a common sight in the Bakery Rat Community, also the Jungle and Storage Communities, to see groups of two or three rats squeaking their favourite anthem and wagging their tails in wild excitement with tears of joy in their eyes. They believed that one day they would be liberated to live their lives as they pleased without oppression and external interference.

Mr Rodent approached the podium for his closing speech before the final onslaught. He cautiously and regally lifted one foot in front of the other, but lurched forwards as he reached the platform. His long tail was wagging with suppressed excitement and he was so proud of Mr Nutty. He finally reached centre stage and stopped, realisation dawning on him that he was at the point where he could witness first hand the gradual fulfilment of their dream.

"Fellow rats and rodents," he thundered. "The elephant's trumpet has sounded, our cup is full and running over. We can no longer continue to absorb this inhuman and obnoxious treatment from those playing God in our lives. Increase your families, sharpen your teeth, drill more burrows, stock your homes, be ready to live rough, sleep rough and play rough. Go the extra mile if you have to... The sun is set and it's time for rat rebellion."

On this note everyone was encouraged to return home and digest what had been said. With a wave of his hands Mr Rodent called it a day and everyone began to disperse with some singing and others humming the new anthem in jubilation.

# CHAPTER NINE

THE LOVELY sunshine of the day met Lord Stephen Kobis and his numerous customers at Bubbles Bubbles wine parlour as they sat in their favourite spots under the large mango tree. They enjoyed the popular African juju music coming from the outdoor loudspeakers hung on the tree and firmly fastened to the trunk.

Richard, Lord Kobis's friend, was on time to narrate a story of what happened in the neighbouring village of Neverland, a stone's throw away from Cayon. A prince went for an early swim in the river with his girlfriend and was drowned when the current swept him into the danger zone. He was not able to save himself while his girlfriend watching from the bank praised and clapped him thinking he was showing off with his antics. It was not until he had not resurfaced for quite a while that she realised there was something seriously wrong and ran to the village crying and shouting for help. Several attempts were made by village lifeguards and fishermen to recover the prince's body, but to no avail. It was eventually discovered floating close to the riverbank by those who had gone to fetch the early morning drinking water.

The terrible news travelled like wildfire and, as Neverland village custom demanded, the prince was buried by the riverbank because his death was perceived as a shameful act of cowardice in the eyes of the gods of the land. The sympathetic elders held a meeting and ordered every member of the village to stop drinking the river water to serve as a punishment to it for drowning their young prince Abokim Nath. He had been very kind and would have been a fitting heir to his father. The people had loved him for being humble and considerate; someone who put others before himself. They all agreed to the use of palm wine as a substitute for the river, it being readily available to all the local villagers.

Two weeks later two dozen villagers had already dropped dead as a result of dehydration, and many more were in hospital in the intensive care unit. Many villagers were soon trekking to the river under cover of darkness to fetch their drinking water, in total defiance of the laws of protest in honour of the late prince, and it was not long before the law makers also joined them calling the ill-fated protest a 'moment of sentimental madness'.

"That is why we are more competent than the people of Neverland village," boasted Lord Kobis, as he raised his right hand to signal an order for more kegs of palm wine for everyone.

The Kija oracular cult had been a family tradition for the Ijayes, which was usually handed down through the generations. The priests were revered because people strongly believed in the efficacy of their secret, potent spiritual powers of divination, spells and magic. The client's spirit had to be in tune with the gods of the Kija Shrine. Kija was a major god of the land who ruled the village of Cayon.

Legend had it that one of the great-grandfathers of Nathan Ijaye, Bolo Ijaye, disappeared in mysterious circumstances as soon as his mother gave birth. A team of village hunters were hired by the family to find him, and it took them seven days of rigorous searching to discover his whereabouts. He was found in the jungle unharmed, lying in the abandoned nest of an ostrich. Bolo was promptly reunited with his shocked family. He was sporting small bands made of cowrie shells, tied around his wrist and waist, a mark of the chosen one of the gods of the land. He was to become a Kija priest.

The family kept a watchful eye on Bolo as he grew, later discovering his special powers that could make certain things happen. By the time he was 11 years old people from near and far visited him to have their problems solved. He often used divination, spells and local herbs for solutions to his clients' worries. It soon became a family tradition for every first male child born into the Ijaye household to automatically become a chosen Kija priest and learn his trade from his forefathers.

It was a laid down rule in the Kija cult that only the spirit of truth prevailed while falsehood had no place in the Kija Shrine, but over the years there had been some sharp practices and the priests ended up paying the bitter price meted out by the gods. Bolo enjoined people to speak the truth during consultations and said that liars were often mysteriously punished by the oracle. Some believed this, but others sneered at his words. When someone stole the wages meant for tribal warriors fighting for Cayon in the intertribal wars, it shook the villagers to the core. The warriors had left their homes, families and loved ones to risk their lives in battle against formidable ethnic rivals from neighbouring villages; the quest for supreme domination in the power struggle. For someone to perpetrate such a deed was something that could not be condoned, for warriors were needed to win battles and take prisoners of war, a hallmark of supremacy.

Bojo was immediately summoned, and every male in Cayon village, young and old, had to drink the sacred water of truth from a secret pond. The water was fetched by Bolo alone, stark naked in the middle of the night. It was taboo for anyone to see him because of the devastating cross-radiation of spiritual power and energy radiating from his body, empowered by the good gods and spirits accompanying him on his clandestine journey. He chanted incantations into the clay pot of sacred water of truth and dipped bunches of young palm fronds into it beneath a giant coconut tree that provided shade and cooled the hallowed stream from which the water was drawn.

A particular market day was fixed for the drinking ritual, and every rat and human member of Cayon village had to be present, in fact the absence of anyone made them a potential suspect. Everyone had to drink from the sacred water to prove their innocence of the theft of the warriors' wages. The result of the ritual would come to light within the following seven days, and sometimes the results for wrongdoers were terrible in both the physical and spiritual sense.

Konja Utek, a young villager who worked as a night guard in the community centre, had not been seen around for some days. His employers had searched for him and reported him to the local police as missing. The village messenger travelled around Cayon with a gong to inform everyone that Konja was missing. The night guard had drunk the sacred water just before his disappearance.

Just as everyone was getting back to normal, Konja returned unannounced with an overblown stomach like an expectant mother of quadruplets. All eyes were turned on him, for every part of his body was swollen out of all proportion as though he was suffering from elephantiasis. He shamelessly headed straight for the Kija Shrine to see high priest Bolo Ijaye to make his confession, after which he mysteriously burst like a punctured balloon. The gods had spoken; he was the culprit and everyone in the village knew it. Custom dictated that no show of respect should be shown, so he had no dignified burial after his despicable act. His scattered remains were gathered into a long cane basket and taken into the jungle where they were left to be devoured by vultures.

The price was also enormous for the family of such a person, as traditional custom demanded that the Kija Shrine was presented with a live bull to pacify the wrath of the gods. This would wipe away the spirit of evil and falsehood as well as cleanse the land that had been spiritually polluted as a result of the theft. The bull was free to wander the entire village and neighbouring villages with only a piece of red ribbon or cloth tied around its neck. This showed that it belonged to the gods of the land and no one should steal or harm it. One guilty of doing so would end the same way as the thief had done. Some believed that feeding the cow would automatically attract a form of blessing from the gods.

If Utek's family was too poor to provide Kija's Shrine with a bull then all hell was let loose on them, the entire family and his bloodline being affected. No one would live to be a ripe old age, every member dying in their prime, and all earthly property of the family would be repossessed as a deterrent to others. Only the sacrifice of a bull to Kija's Shrine would pacify the awesome power of the gods.

Many consulted the priests, Mayor Dan Dakota among them in his quest to rule the City of Canterborne forever – his driving factor. Papa Nathan Ijaye, the great-grandson of the late Bolo and a successor to the Kija Shrine, was living in the remote village of Cayon. He was a hired hand of Mayor Dakota to ensure his victory in the coming election, his main duty being to incapacitate the mayor's political opponents using witchcraft and voodoo in any way he could. It was hoped that in the confusion, Mayor Dakota could hoodwink the electorate and gain a landslide victory. Nathan was promised a lump sum in payment for services rendered.

Papa Nathan Ijaya narrated a story to Mayor Dan Dakota, which had been handed down to him by his ancestors in the days of Bolo Ijaya.

A married woman became pregnant by a man who was not her husband. Her suspicious husband dragged her to Bolo Kija's Shrine where she was requested to speak the truth about the father of her unborn child. She insisted it was her husband's and was eventually made to drink the sacred water of truth to prove her innocence.

On the morning of the seventh day, as she was hurrying to the village spring she fell and her stomach burst, revealing a stillborn baby. With no none around to help, she died shortly afterwards, her body being discovered later that morning by those returning from the spring. At the other end of the neighbouring village of Koika, her secret lover was working on his farm making furrows in preparation for the next farming season. He was working beneath a palm tree when a large coconut fell, hitting him hard on his bare head and crushing his skull – he died on the spot. The news travelled fast and both bodies were taken to the Kija Shrine together with their belongings and two local bulls, the expected present for the gods as atonement for their atrocious relationship. In the village of Cayon, the list of such victims was endless in the days of Bolo Ijaye, according to Papa Nathan.

As a result of his commitment to the Kija gods, and as the most powerful cult priest in Cayon, Papa Nathan Ijaye did not find it difficult to tell Mayor Dakota to be fair in all his dealings, but the mayor always expected a magic wand approach to every issue and would not have it any other way. He was determined to win the coming election at all costs and nothing would stand in his way including Papa Nathan's stupid claim of fairness when nature itself was never fair. He did not care really as the priest had promised to help him and his hands were clean anyway. He returned from the consultation with a smile on his face, but had got the wrong end of the stick.

The mayor embarked on another serious spending spree, buying expensive cars and other gifts for the human and rat citizens of the City of Canterbourne, to be given to those who joined the rally as he canvassed for votes. His political speeches contained nothing new or meaningful, however, many returned home with brand new vehicles or expensive gifts, but others returned empty-handed, although full of hope and promises. Mayor Dan Dakota cared little for the citizens of the rural villages surrounding his city.

Mr Kalio O'Brien concentrated on the rural villages quite unaware of the fact that the entire rat population was leaving no stone unturned to canvass for him. Those who were brave enough to enter the city to canvass for votes did so under cover of darkness to minimise casualty and reprisals by Mayor Dakota's loyalists. The rats' slogan, written and thought up by Mr Rodent, was, 'Vote for O'Brien, vote for truth, vote for change, vote for conscience, materialism is deceptive!', which was scribbled on tiny pieces of paper so that everyone had a copy reminding them what to do.

Mr Rodent secretly requested that everyone collect whatever gifts Mayor Dakota and his men offered, because those bribes actually belonged to the citizens of Canterborne, so he was only giving them a percentage of that which he had stolen from them. These gifts were the products of their sweat and toil, so he was not doing anyone any favours.

Mayor Dan Dakota had already eliminated those candidates whom he felt would be strong opponents, during a trumped up coup alarm, and the remaining opposition did not seem enough of a threat to his political ambition. Anyway, they had been dealt with by the systematic clipping of their financial powers, disrupting their businesses with endless bureaucratic bottleness so that no funds were left for political ambition. After assessing the situation, the mayor was convinced that only he could win the election with no hassle and there was no reason why he could not be in office forever.

Mayor Dakota's wife, Nancia Abdul, always found one excuse or another to paint the town red by throwing expensive parties. She was a woman about town who loved money, the good life and showing off her husband's wealth. She thought donating to charitable causes was a sheer waste of time and money and could not understand those who went cap in hand begging for favours. When not partying, she was enjoying herself on endless vacations in choice worldwide locations and engrossed in shopping sprees. She was on first-name terms with Versace, Gucci and Armani amongst other fashion designers. Settling down and having a normal family life was definitely not on her agenda.

Nancia confided in a friend that she thought her husband would remain in office forever, so there would be enough time and money to throw around for a very long time. She also said Papa Nathan Ijaye had been added to their list of witch doctors, marabouts and sorcerers, so there was no way they would lose the election with his backing.

"He is the best in the land, but what worries me is his insistence of fairness…" Nancy told Lucy Tayan, a close friend. "He must have a price, everyone does. We'll find out his price tag and win him over completely."

Some weeks later, Nancia Abdul Dakota visited Papa Nathan Ijaye in Cayon village. He told her the story he had told her husband about the cheating married woman who became pregnant by another man. He told her how she had been made to drink the sacred water of truth and what had happened. When he had finished, Nancia thanked Papa for his wisdom and the story.

"Papa, this is politics we are talking about, not morality," she said.

Later she presented the priest with a bundle of beautifully wrapped gifts. No one knew what they were, but they were accepted with good grace. On leaving, she reminded him of the coming election, but Papa merely nodded and wished her well, then she left with her entourage of bodyguards, disappeared into the waiting car and was driven off at great speed.

Mr Jingo, the new spy mouse in the mayor's residence, overheard a conversation about a planned foreign trip to New York, USA, arranged for a few weeks later, to attend an international conference on the improvement of the nation's economy. Mayor Dan Dakota was to be a spokesman on that occasion. The mayor hired the foremost professor of economics from a leading university in the city to deliver the speech for him, hoping that his good presentation would convince the world leaders that all was well in Canterborne and the neighbouring towns and villages.

Jingo happened to be in the right place at the right time, namely Dan Dakota's lounge, so he remembered the conversation so that he could share it with Mr Rodent as soon as possible. When the coast was clear, he sneaked out and was soon back in the Bakery Rat Community relating the good news.

# CHAPTER TEN

LORD STEPHEN Kobis, real name Stephen Elgar-James, was British, having been born in the remote countryside of Tenbury Wells, Worcestershire. He grew up as a typical, British country boy with a loving family of four. His father was a local farmer who grew Irish potatoes and owned a sizeable ranch house where he bred horses for trade. Young Stephen loved his father's business and, as a result, was often the needed, extra hand feeding and caring for the animals. He also assisted in gathering and rolling the hay and silage from the fields, which was compacted and stored for the horses' winter feed.

Stephen's mother, Janice Elgar-James, loved and cared for her husband and the two young lads, Stephen and Luke. Luke was the eldest, the exact opposite of his brother, being somewhat of a rebel whose only interests were mountain climbing and surfing. He disliked horses and often groaned when his father sent him on an errand such as to fetch the vet or shoe and feed them.

Stephen loved and cherished Tenbury Wells, especially in the summer when tourists would arrive on vacation. He never stopped boasting about his beloved countryside and loved his quiet cycle rides along narrow pathways on his mountain bike. Visitors often approached him for directions, and he was only too pleased to help, politely explaining about the interesting places in the vicinity like the River Teme, Royal Hunters' Walks, Bromyard Heritage Centre, the West Midland Safari and Leisure Park and Elgar's Birthplace Museum. He encouraged them to visit the nearby towns of Kidderminster and Worcester, rambling on and on until they had to make excuses that they must be off. They would drive away to their booked accommodation amazed at the young man's zeal and helpfulness; someone who obviously cared a great deal about his countryside home.

The seven-year-old boy loved being in the company of his father, and they often explored the countryside together. The River Teme was a favourite haunt, especially where it flowed from the Kerry Hills above Knighton to join the River Severn at Powick. Some tourists thought the river valley was spoilt, but its peace and tranquillity denied this. Once a month, father and son went to a very successful farmers' market at The Talbot, Knightwick, to sell their Irish potatoes and purchase fresh local ingredients then they enjoyed a picnic on their return journey. Such childhood experiences went a long way in preparing the young Stephen Elgar-James for his future, and also the fact that he was brought up in such a close-knit neighbourhood.

"Be prepared for whatever life throws at you, son," his father advised.

Stephen's father taught him to be tolerant of others' culture, beliefs, opinions and ways of life.

"You don't force people to change, for change itself leads the way," said his father.

Stephen loved bird watching, another pastime he shared with his father. They would often go to the Malvern Hills, an area of outstanding natural beauty and one teeming with a diverse habitat for many species of birds. They would listen to the bird calls of the skylark, snipe, woodpecker and kestrel as they echoed around the hills. They saw dragonflies and rare butterflies and, around the wet areas, common geese amongst the rough grasses. Very often they came across cows and sheep grazing in the valley and even deer in the early morning or evening peace of the environment.

On evening walks or cycle rides after a hard day's work, Stephen spied badgers and foxes; creatures that lived secretly in the woods. He saw telltale signs of badgers' hairs hanging from wire or deer footprints in the mud, and also smelled the musty scent of a fox hanging in the still evening air. Chewed nuts scattered around told him of squirrels, mice and voles, the dormice and squirrels often foraging high in the trees in search of hazelnuts.

One day Stephen was cycling home on the bike he had been given for his tenth birthday when he came across a badger struggling for its life at the side of the road. It had been knocked down by a careless driver, so the lad made the immediate decision to pick up the gasping and bleeding animal, put it into his bicycle basket and take it to the nearest veterinary clinic about a quarter of a mile away. The vet took the animal's pulse and pronounced it dead. It was at that time that a very sad and weeping Stephen promised himself he would lead a campaign against hit-and-run drivers, and poachers of defenceless creatures.

His school vacation came to an end and he had to return to Worcester College where he was studying the sciences. Later he studied mechanical engineering at university and, as a result, his campaign had to be put on hold due to serious academic commitments. He later graduated from Cambridge University with a degree in mechanical engineering, taking up the position of engineer with Rock Oil International, a multinational oil company in Holland. Stephen was eventually transferred to the City of Canterborne off-shore department where he operated as a team leader on an oil rig just off the coast of Cayon village.

Despite his privileged Western upbringing, Stephen was quick to adapt to the culture and way of life of the natives. He absorbed their traditions, and could often be found drinking palm wine with the locals in Bubbles Bubbles wine parlour. He enjoyed chatting to the residents of Cayon and sharing their lifestyle. He loved their rawness and closeness to nature, everything being devoid of racial prejudice. His upbringing in Tenbury Wells had greatly succeeded in preparing him for the new life fate had thrown at his feet.

"The locals respect and accept you for whom you are, not judging your colour, but the goodness in your heart," Stephen told Richard Josty, a close friend who had emigrated from his Jamaican homeland to settle in Cayon after retiring from the Black Gold Oil Company.

Richard had bought a permanent home and settled down amongst the natives, spending his retirement money to establish a cattle ranch and goat-rearing business just like his friend. He employed many local workers and ensured that they were well paid by village standards.

Stephen met Catherine, the first daughter of High Chief Laz Okonta, the community leader of Cayon, at a child naming ceremony. It was love at first sight, their friendship growing and developing into a marriage union. Many believed it would not work out due to cultural differences, but they were later to become the envy of all. Stephen met all the traditional marriage rites and bride price of his in-laws and even flew his parents over from England to attend the wonderful occasion. They were later blessed with two beautiful daughters.

High Chief Laz Okonta honoured Stephen with the prized chieftancy title of 'Lord Kobis', which meant, 'he has come to stay'. He was extremely proud of his official title, Lord Stephen Kobis, as he was now a lord and elder of the land of Cayon village. He employed a first-class schoolteacher to instruct him in the local language and was soon proficient enough to be able to speak and write in the native language. He often flaunted this acquisition during communal elders' meetings to the admiration of all.

Stephen finally retired from active service with the oil company and decided to buy extensive acreage for his home, stables and a pig farm.

"He is now one of us," said one of the oldest chiefs during a cabinet meeting, as he broke kola nuts and poured libation to usher in the new yam festival season.

"Thank you very much, Chief Pascal Obudu, but man is man whatever his colour," Stephen replied.

He was decked out in full, crimson, flamboyant chieftaincy regalia as he took his seat among the elders and lawmakers of Cayon village to celebrate the yam festival amidst pomp and ceremony – he was beaming broadly.

"As for me and my household, we've left everything for God to sort out," said Mr Rodent as he entered his bathroom to enjoy a cold bath.

The leaders of the Storage Rat Community were in close touch with Mr Rodent, secretly meeting to discuss issues of importance regarding their continuous survival in the City of Canterborne and the surrounding area.

"There is no way he can lose this election," emphasised Benjamin Okot, a villager from the south of Canterborne, as he chatted to his friend, Peter Lemar. "Not after all this massive expenditure on gifts and impromptu charitable gestures to the high and mighty in the city and abroad. I heard he recently made a donation of a private jet to Chief Kakoro Ubaka, the community leader of Onigo, one of the major oil producing communities south of Canterborne, to help win his people over to his camp."

Most of the human and rat citizens of Canterborne seemed to have been keeping a close watch on the general activities of Mayor Dan Dakota and his political allies as they geared themselves up for the election. He used his wealth to lure many onto his side and everyone began to believe he would be in office for a long time since there seemed to be no contender to match his wealth.

One of Lord Stephen Kobis's trusty horses had just won a great race and the owner was soon back at Bubbles Bubbles, the melting pot of the rich and poor.

Stephen's wife had died two years previously leaving him with two lovely daughters who were now law graduates from Cambridge University, England. They were home on vacation to spend time with their father whom they both adored. He had refused to remarry because he had loved Catherine so much and believed no other could qualify for her place in his heart. He was frightened of being robbed of her memory. He often told Caroline, his eldest daughter, that he could see her mother in her in almost every way. His other daughter took after her father, the shrewd businessman.

Stephen had retired from active politics after losing money and business to Mayor Dakota, who hated political rivalry or strong opposition of any kind. He had then decided to move into a new venture far removed from the political scene - bookies, pigs, horses and training.

Everyone sat around the bamboo table at Bubbles Bubbles under the large mango tree. There were many customers because it was the weekend. Richard Josty was on hand to tell another story of a man who lost his only son to one of the so-called vigilante groups around Canterborne. The man was summoned to the house of worship to bless his dead son before burial.

"You are all welcome to this farewell service for our lovely friend, brother and son. There are numerous houses of worship in today's society and one can only hope they are all doing the right thing. As we bid Kevin farewell today, we believe that one day we shall meet him in paradise in the heavens with God, our Creator-"

"Wait a minute," interrupted Bryan, Kevin's father. "I

have a couple of hard questions for God. I wonder if he
will ever be able to give me good enough reasons for taking away my son, and why there is so much injustice…"

He was still kicking and shouting at the top of his voice,
disrupting the service, as he was led away by friends and
family who shared his sorrow, to calm down.

"It's all about faith," Stephen said, as he ordered more
drinks and Caroline wiped palm wine foam from his
moustache with her handkerchief.

Zero hour finally arrived and, to the surprise of many,
Mr Kalio O'Brien, the bakery owner, won the election with
a massive landslide victory. The electorate had finally listened to and obeyed their conscience by voting against
Dan Dakota and his moneybag friends and cronies, shun-
ning wealth and materialism for principles and the voice
of reason. The poll proved that the rats and human citizens
of the City of Canterborne had spoken their mind and it
was now clear who called the shots. Mayor Dan Dakota
shamefully relinquished his office for the newly sworn in
Mayor Kalio O'Brien.

Everyone thought it was a dream come true, for they
now had a new leader who would take care of them and
listen to them. Their secret manoeuvres and dedication
had finally paid off, however, they had to keep watch and
pray that Mayor O'Brien did not disappoint them. They
knew very well that power could corrupt and go to his
head.

Most of Dan Dakota's followers had voted for Kalio
O'Brien because they wanted real change. They chose the
path of truth and followed their hearts, their stand being very clear to the ex mayor. Without political author-
ity, Dakota was powerless, and a committee was quickly
formed to make him and his men account for how they
looted the nation's treasury. Most of them, including Dan
Dakota, were arrested and detained in the maximum security prison so they could not flee the city and cross the

border. They were left there to cool off until the national auditing committee had finished their job.

Nancia, Dakota's wife, was one of the lucky ones, who fled to the Caribbean islands and her holiday home. She had quietly left on the eve of the election as if she had a premonition of the result. On hearing that Kalio O'Brien had become the new mayor she was quick to declare her absolute loyalty to him, even phoning him from her Caribbean hideout. With enough ill-gotten gains and fat bank accounts off-shore in the Bahamas and the Caribbean, Nancia made it clear to Dakota that their marriage was over - it had died with his loss of power.

Close friends who had attended their flamboyant wedding, remembered her words and fitted the missing piece of the jigsaw.

"For better, mine darling; for worse, I've gone for good and I'm not coming back."

# CHAPTER ELEVEN

O NE BRIGHT sunny morning Mr Rodent awoke with a start, only to find that his wife and son had disappeared and all efforts to locate them proved fruitless.

He stood at the entrance to his burrow gazing at the sky, trying to clear the cobwebs of thousands of conflicting thoughts that were streaming into his oval head. It soon dawned on him that he might never see his family again; he might have lost them forever. The one million dollar question stuck in his mind was how to get a clue as to what incident had transpired to bring about such a tragedy. He just could not figure out a relevant answer and as his thoughts strayed he remembered some uneaten nuts in the corner of his lounge. He decided to sneak in and take a bite.

No sooner had he returned inside when he heard a loud bang on the door and Mrs Messy entered. She specialised in rummaging through rubbish heaps scavenging for the smallest meal.

"I'm sorry Mr Rodent. Please accept my sympathy," she said. "I narrowly escaped death by a whisker. It all happened last night when your wife and son met me at the new rubbish tip by the railway station near City Hall. An unmistakable odour hung in the air, one that a rat in his right mind could not ignore. It was the unique fragrance of smoked crayfish and nut meal, in fact I was ready to trade one of my limbs for it. Before anyone could say, 'What a nice meal!' your wife and son were at it. I joined them to have a bite when all of a sudden we heard a loud bang and they were imprisoned in a huge trap set by God knows who. I'm deeply sorry to say your family died a few seconds later, such a painful way to lose them."

Is that so? thought Mr Rodent. I'm yet another victim of those stupid humans. I must get to the bottom of this and seek my revenge no matter how long it takes.

The following evening before midnight, Mr Rodent was already at the rubbish tip hiding inside an empty tar drum that had been discarded after the recent roadworks. He sat there quietly trying to figure out which human was responsible for the deaths of his wife and son. There were some who were fond of emptying waste bins at the site at night to avoid detection and the heavy hand of the environmental laws. He did not have to wait long before the city's mayor pulled up in his minivan with the back open and within minutes his men were quickly dragging several rubbish-laden bin bags onto the dump. This all went on as the mayor sat at the wheel of the vehicle ready to make a quick getaway.

"Check those traps," thundered Mayor O'Brien.

"Nothing this time," Johnny replied.

"OK, hop in and let's go. The rat population in this community is too high, so we have to eliminate them all," the mayor said, starting the engine and driving off.

Convinced that they were out of sight, Mr Rodent scurried home with thousands of angry thoughts flooding his mind.

# CHAPTER TWELVE

A NEW ERA had begun in the lives of the human and rat citizens of the City of Canterborne, ushered in by the election of Mayor Kalio O'Brien.

The rats residing in the Bakery Rat Community swore never to evacuate the countless secret corners and hiding places, for they had embarked on endless reproduction exercises to swell their numbers and continue the fight where their elders had left off. Mayor O'Brien was a man of great traditional prowess and intelligence who at first saw no reason why the rats should not be left alone to live their rugged lives as they pleased, hence his indifference to their activities.

The City of Canterborne shared borders with several rural communities that seemed to have little to do with the urban centre's way of life. Sometimes the women were seen, and the men invaded the city with their annual harvest produced from their fertile land, such as wheat, groundnuts, cereal and even poultry.

Manatee, O'Brien's wife, and their only daughter, Anita, ensured that good quality produce was purchased for bread production. Numerous jobless young men and women were employed in the bakery on low wages, to ensure that people had jobs and food. There had been a remarkably high rate of unemployment due to the economic slump in the city.

Mayor O'Brien sat behind his huge office desk pondering how he had come to move from Cayon village to the city in search of greener pastures. His bakery business had fallen on hard times economically and he had become so indebted to suppliers that he had been made bankrupt. One morning he awoke to find that his entire staff had left, as they could no longer continue to hear his excuses about hardship and non-payment of their wages. Their unpaid bills were piling up, so the decision to leave was the wisest. As a result, he had to relocate, ending up in the City of Canterborne with Manatee and Anita. He had no idea that some uninvited rats had stowed away in drawers and other luggage to surprise him.

His small branch of the bakery in the city was doing well at that time, but not well enough. With a pregnant wife, very little income and accommodation worries it was a very trying time for Kalio O'Brien. He decided to convert his small bakery by partitioning it off, thus giving the family a small bakery and living quarters. He had to let his only staff member go and took up the challenge of running the place single-handedly. He worked painstakingly until he had his breakthrough, which had not been handed to him on a golden platter, but achieved through sweat, toil and suffering.

Several years later, what had started as a game on the part of the stowaway rats, emerged as something very formidable. The rats had been on the increase, and a visit to the bakery store would have stunned anyone. They strolled around, engrossed in whatever mischief was at hand, daring anyone to attack or question their integrity. They looked upon the place as their home; a home to be guarded jealously and an unapproved inheritance to die for.

Owing to Mr O'Brien's business acumen, the family moved to larger premises to befit his new status. He employed more staff and now won the election to the office of Mayor of Canterborne.

The former mayor, Dan Dakota, had committed suicide after his wife left him for a younger man. He could not cope with the pain and decided to end it all. After a three-day intensive search, his body was found by a fisherman of Zimako. Dakota had a heavy object tied around his neck with a thick cord. It was rumoured that before his demise he had met his solicitors to change his will in favour of the state with a proviso that Nancia was never to be allowed to see his body.

A few months after the election, Mayor O'Brien was living away from his bakery, leaving it to the rats who were a common sight there, competing for food and space. As time passed, people began to complain about the rats' activities in the City of Canterborne, all fingers pointing at the mayor because of his neglect and carefree attitude, which had led to the influx of the vermin.

"Had he stepped in before now, this calamity could have been stemmed," Mr Heartless pointed out to the cabinet members.

It was an open secret that the mayor's household was breeding rats, and their nefarious activities were fast spreading to other homes in the city. People complained of this social nuisance. It was reported that some playgroup children's fingers had been bitten off by greedy rats, mistaking the digits for pieces of cake. It was said that one boy was coming down the stairs when he saw a rat scampering away with a piece of cake his mother had given him. Picking up the robust creature, he rushed outside to show his friends, but before he got there two fingers had been bitten off. He dropped the rat and it quickly disappeared down the nearest hole. Reports of such incidents were endless.

Mr Rodent was one of the surviving sons of the early settlers of the Bakery Rat Community who successfully relocated to the City of Canterborne with Mayor Kalio O'Brien's household in those trying days. He was a very intelligent rat who knew when to hang on and when to let go, never complicating issues. He was a sociable character who interacted with the jungle rats despite his exalted position as one of the insiders in the mayor's bakery.

The jungle rats struggled to survive in their hostile environment, especially when it came to finding food. They had to learn how to negotiate the numerous disguised traps just waiting in the wings for unsuspecting rodents. Just going out and arriving home safely was a bonus and they were never too sure if they would live to tell the tale of their adventurous escapades. They were wary of some predators like Mr Snake and his family, cats and the mongoose, for they liked nothing better than a tasty rat.

Luckily for Mr Rodent in the Bakery Rat Community, food was always on tap. He only had to stroll into the storeroom, use his strong teeth to bite open a bag and feast on the contents. All he cared about was the resident rats being well fed and not the fact that they were diminishing the mayor's bread and butter! The bags riddled with holes created much waste, a cause of concern to the bakery staff who reported the fact to their employer. Initially it was no big deal to the mayor, but now the situation was getting out of hand and required urgent attention, especially as there had been numerous complaints about the rat menace in the City of Canterborne.

Residents of the Bakery Rat Community were the envy of all, for they enjoyed a secure family life unlike their jungle friends who could hardly sleep for fear of marauders and predators who attacked when they least suspected it. Life in the jungle was very tough. The bakery rats only allowed jungle rats to live with them through marriage.

The rats in the bakery had escape routes, which was just as well when Mayor O'Brien's men started brandishing sticks and other weapons of destruction. The rats had no choice but to flee their homes, but hundreds were slaughtered.

Mr Rodent often thought of the past and one particular occasion when he had visited the jungle. As a result, he had met and married his late wife then brought her to live in the bakery. Months rolled by and they had a son who unfortunately learned the destructive art of vandalism and mischief. He would burst the cereal sacks and, at times, defecate in the mixing bowls without a care in the world. He defiantly brought his jungle mates to the bakery, flouting all the rules, wreaking havoc and leaving telltale signs of their riotous presence. No one dared to question him because his father was a loved and respected leader of the community who seemed to turn a blind eye to his son's behaviour. This behaviour continued until that fateful day when he and his mother had met a tragic death in the mousetrap at the rubbish tip, as related to Mr Rodent by Mrs Messy.

Mrs Messy had been an early settler, who was now in charge of environmental neatness in the community. Her position included keeping the rats' burrows clean at all times, making sure no one defecated in the living rooms and checking security, raising the alarm when there was any suspicion of an intruder. The rats thought it complimentary to relieve themselves inside and on top of the cereal bags, for they were just lying around full of food that no one could possibly eat in a lifetime. Each rat marked out its own territory, a no go area to other families unless they were friends.

Mrs Messy was a notorious gossip; whatever she saw or heard was grossly exaggerated. On one occasion she caused the untimely death of her dear husband by telling the community that he was planning to overthrow the incumbent leader, which was said to settle the score and punish him after a gruelling night of rows. What started as a game ended up with Mr Messy being executed by the power-drunk leadership of the day who did not want anyone to topple them from their exalted position in the rat kingdom.

Every rat had learned how to deal with Mrs Messy and, at one point, some families barred her from visiting their homes whilst others made sure no family secrets were revealed when she did. They wanted her to leave immediately after pleasantries had been exchanged, for it was rumoured that the walls had ears and could report back to her whatever was said about her.

She made sure everybody heard of the tragic death of Mr Rodent's family, despite the fact that he had asked her to keep it a secret to have time to mourn his loss quietly whilst still conducting a personal investigation.

The rats' menace in the City of Canterborne finally came to a head when the human citizens could no longer tolerate the malicious atrocities in their homes. There were pockets of protest that led to a march and mass gathering at Mayor O'Brien's residence.

Mayor O'Brien had just woken up with a start and gone to the bathroom for his morning ablutions in preparation for the day's tasks. Never in the history of the community had he ever been awakened so early in the day. Something must be seriously wrong, he thought. Protesters had started to pour into his compound and he had no idea that a group of community leaders were already seated in his lounge waiting for him. He sent his wife to inform those waiting that he would soon join them then dressed hurriedly.

On seeing his visitors, the mayor was shocked that everybody was pointing accusing fingers at him and his household for introducing rats into the community. The rodents had taken over and were leaving rubbish everywhere, he was told.

Mr Stewart, the community planner, bitterly explained how his wedding suit, purchased for his daughter's wed-

ding, had been torn to shreds by rats that had even urinated on it. He showed the ruined suit to the gathering
and there was a general show of resentment from shocked
and bewildered citizens.

"Enough is enough!" was the cry that rent the air.

Mr Pepper, the community food merchant, stood up
defiantly.

"Enough is enough! I can't take it any more. Last month
I spent a lot of money stocking my warehouse with various bags and sacks of food items to sell, but when I went
there yesterday I got the shock of my life. Every bag I
lifted up to take to my customers had holes in it and the
grain rained upon the floor. Very soon the entire warehouse floor was covered in a sea of different grain, beans
and rice all mixed up. Now I'm on the verge of losing the
numerous customers I've had for years, and to win back
their trust won't be easy. I can no longer meet their orders
and they could turn to my business rivals, which would
be a disaster. This is the gripe I have with such vermin and
I can't wait to roast them alive. If I could lay my hands on
them…"

Mr Pepper sat down fuming with uncontrollable rage
as Manatee, the mayor's wife, told of how she had been
sitting in the lounge the previous week before watching
an interesting film on the television, only to sense that
something was moving beneath the cover of the sofa. She
had stood up to check the silent movement only to find
a fat mother rat scampering out of the sofa followed by
her child who could not keep up with her. She caught the
young rat for extermination, but by then the sofa was ruined. It was riddled with thousands of holes and the wood
and material had been bundled up into a heap – the invad-
ing rat had made it into her maternity home. The sofa was
now undergoing extensive repair in the furniture work-
shop. The list of complaints went on and on.

As deliberations continued on how to tackle the rat issue, Mr Rascal was hidden in a dark corner in the mayor's lounge, eavesdropping on all that was said by the 'naughty humans', as the rats often referred to them. He promised himself that Mr Rodent would hear everything they were planning to wreak havoc in the rat community in the not too distant future, especially as he had taken a great risk to be there as a witness. As the meeting ended, Mr Rascal raced off to inform Mr Rodent of the humans' plans, and his leader was very grateful, promising to match the plans come what may.

Mr Rodent immediately summoned a midnight meeting in the mixing room at the bakery via Mr Loudmouth and Mrs Messy, who informed the entire rat community of the impending war with the humans. A notice appeared in a popular spot. It was scratched out and everyone who saw it immediately knew it was one of Mrs Messy's, due to the lopsidedness of the letters.

No scouting tonight
all must be present at a most important meeting
midnight – mixing room

A supreme rat council chaired by Mr Rodent, consisting of five major members, three rats and two mice, was quickly inaugurated. They went underground to prepare for the all-important meeting.

# CHAPTER THIRTEEN

**M**AYOR O'BRIEN'S bakery was situated midway between the City of Canterborne and the farm settlements on the outskirts of the city. He no longer lived within the large compound, leaving it to his staff to continue the bread production and report back to him.

The resident rat community did not bother the staff until their antics became nauseating and intolerable in the bakery and the city. The workers often used the destructive nature and looting of the rats to cover up their nefarious activities of pilfering bags and sacks of cereal at night. When things went missing it was convenient to blame everything on the rats when the mayor asked questions, and they were never caught. They constantly demanded money to restock the storeroom, and the little profit they made was enough to make them close their eyes to the real evil of the rats' invasion. Little did they know that the mayor had been in the bakery business long enough to know how long his stock normally lasted, so he was beginning to have his suspicions.

After questioning the staff, the mayor came to the conclusion that the rats were the culprits, but saw no reason to decimate them as they were part of a beautiful world and obviously had to eat. He thought people should make allowances for this fact and, looking at the size of a rat's mouth and tummy, he was sure it could not eat that much anyway. He only visited the bakery once a week due to a very busy schedule, and when he did he never came into contact with rats, but saw the telltale signs of their handiwork.

Eventually, under much pressure from the citizens, and after a last check on his stock, he decided something had to be done to stem the increasing number of rats. They had spread into the city causing trouble and wrecking homes, and he was being blamed, so the battle lines were drawn.

The bakery consisted of a large bungalow with many wooden partitions, the largest room being the bakery section containing the bread making machinery. There was also a smaller storeroom, referred to as the 'strong room' by the staff, but the rats called it the 'dining section'! The other rooms served as temporary staff accommodation, especially for those working the night shift. There was also a small secluded bungalow used as an office by the mayor, his secretary and cashier. This was where all trade and transactions took place.

Mayor O'Brien called the bakery 'The Cayon Park' because that was where it had all begun – his journey from rags to riches.

With each passing day, the handwriting on the wall became clearer to the Bakery Rat Community. The bakery staff were becoming violent towards them, sometimes injuring their wives and children.

"This is quite unacceptable," thundered Mr Rascal, head of the rat planning committee.

He pointed out the injuries sustained by one of his sons who happened to be indoors at the time of a stick attack, when one of the bakery staff had prodded their burrow. He concluded that something should definitely be done to forestall any future occurrence.

He contacted Mr Rodent, who was still enduring the

agonising loss of his wife and child. They sat down to deliberate before inviting others, and came to the conclusion that war between the human leaders and rat community was imminent. A midnight meeting was set and the venue arranged; Mayor O'Brien's staff and neighbours would be fast asleep then if they were at home, for they often visited family in the city at weekends. The rats hoped this would avoid human intrusion of any kind.

The Bakery Rat Community intended to involve the jungle rats to muster support, even though they were not the best of friends, but at such times any friend would do, especially as their precious home was threatened. Some said that when the going gets tough, the tough get going, and Mrs Messy said they should be their brother's keeper, conveniently forgetting how she used to bully the jungle rats at the annual party.

On the night of the meeting everyone scurried to the designated venue. Mr Rodent and Mr Rascal were the first to arrive, others came in twos and threes and soon everyone had gathered for the great deliberation. Mr Rodent was the first to speak.

"Fellow rats, I start by thanking you all for being present, and for your determination to make this a great occasion. It has often been said that when you see a frog frantically jumping about in broad daylight be rest assured that if he is not after something, then something must be after him. Fellow rats, to say that all is well with us at present in the Bakery Rat Community is madness, and if that is said it can be likened to the liar who claimed to have sown thousands of carrots, but at harvest time he will surely harvest a thousand lies. When a child is in distress, crying and pointing his finger, be rest assured he is really beckoning for someone to fight his battles for him.

We are all aware that our stay and existence in the Bakery Rat Community is fast drawing to a close if recent developments are anything to go by. There has been a serious and calculated attempt by the human community to deprive us of our good life here in the bakery. The time has come to put our heads together and make a reasoned decision. As you are aware, I lost my family in one fell swoop, only God knows if I will ever recover from that, but to dispossess us of our lovely homes they will have to kill us first. My people, what are your options?"

He sat down to let his words sink in and allow Mr Rascal to put forward his views.

"Fellow rats and mice, I am asking us if we have lost the will and courage to fight and defend ourselves in the face of the human enemy."

As he sat down, Mrs Messy rose to her feet.

"Fellow rats and rodents, what are we waiting for? I've already lost my husband so nothing else can scare me now. Right now I suggest we set up a defence committee to really tackle this issue before we are all murdered in our sleep. Thank you," she thundered, amid thunderous applause.

Mr Rodent appointed Mr Rascal, Mr Loudmouth and Mr Naughty to form a sub-committee, put their heads together and come up with a strategy. The meeting closed and everyone dispersed in the wee hours of the morning before the usual activities of each morning in the Bakery Rat Community began.

# CHAPTER FOURTEEN

MR RODENT sat in his chair, rhythmically rocking to and fro as he remembered how he had learned his first lessons as a child when Mayor O'Brien used to help Anita with her alphabet and numbers.

In those days Messy, Rascal and Rodent had been young and intelligent with a burning desire to learn. They had often strolled around picking up bits and pieces of discarded educational materials, at the same time listening to how Mr O'Brien used the alphabet. They heard Anita and her father singing. 'Baa baa black sheep have you any wool' at the end of the lesson, with Anita using her pencil to tap out the rhythm on the table. This all made the three friends more determined to learn the 'human magic'.

Mr Rodent thought about how Mr O'Brien had never bothered with the rats in those days, ignoring their presence and concentrating on his business most of the time. He began to wonder how everything had changed so quickly as the rat population had increased. At least he could now read and write a little, although not on the human scale, but being able to do what little he could was better than nothing. Being able to achieve some human accomplishments had at least made it easy for him to hold sway in the rat community.

He tried to fathom out the way humans reasoned – one

day they were friendly and happy, the next sad, moody and even dangerous, throwing things to cause harm. He could not see that as a game, so he and others had re-solved to hide, for the less humans saw of them the better. His wandering thoughts recalled how he had lost touch with his parents and siblings back in Cayon when he had unexpectedly relocated to Canterbourne with O'Brien. It had come as a great shock, for he had not known that he would wake up one day and have to continue his life in the city. It was not until he had looked around that he had discovered that Rascal and Messy had also been victims of the move, but they all agreed they were there in search of greener pastures, but there was always the nagging un-answered question, 'At whose expense?'. It was obvious that they would not see their parents again, for it was re-corded that those who had not wished to leave their hard-earned businesses in Cayon and had tried to escape whilst O'Brien's men were packing had been brutally murdered.

As Mr Rodent travelled down memory lane he thought of June, his ill-fated wife. As he closed his eyes, ponder-ing over what the future held for him, it all came flooding back in a flash; the incident that had left him devastated in those terrible agonising days. He had actually had a large family of seven and their life story changed the day they all went for a short vacation to spend time with a very close jungle friend in the village of Nupee. The journey took a day as they had to swim across the mighty River Mangu, the currents of which could be very dangerous and unpredictable. Only the brave dared cross it.

Mr Rodent and his family had set out in the early hours of the morning carrying nuts in their mouths in case they felt peckish along the way.

"We should not use the long bridge as we don't want to bump into any crazy humans," June said.

They all agreed to use the rat routes in the jungle avoid-ing humans' tar roads and cars, and they would swim

across the river to the other side where they would continue their journey. It would be tricky, but the family were
strong swimmers. Mr Rodent plunged into the River
Mangu first after advising the rest to follow in single file
each firmly clamping their teeth onto the tail of the one in
front. They were also to use their fore and hind limbs to
push the water backwards to propel themselves forwards.
The arrangement was perfect and they soon found themselves crossing the river. Once on dry land they spread
themselves out in the sun to dry their wet bodies, each
chewing on their store of nuts as it was already nearly
midday. Having rested for a few hours they resumed their
journey following the familiar jungle tracks.

As they arrived, Mr Konky saw them in the distance
and sent his sons to give the family a proper welcome, a
rat tradition for a valued friendship. Mr Konky lived in
a remote village called Harlom, a very tough, rat mafia
neighbourhood with stubborn rat families. Several years
previously as a young rat, he had made his home in the
village and had often gone with his father, Atek, now a
blessed memory, to people's farms on dark nights. They
had been known for the aggressiveness and mindlessness
with which they attacked and plundered farm produce
such as potatoes, beans, ripe plantain, corn and wheat.

Those owners whose farms had been unlucky enough
to be visited told horrific stories, so much so that they set
traps to catch the perpetrators and teach a bitter lesson
to others. Atek was an unfortunate victim of such a trap
after his long years of adventures and escapades, making Konky an orphan at a very tender age, having lost his
mother a few years earlier. Villagers knew the boy and his
exploits only too well, but the problem was catching him
red-handed, and he had vowed not to suffer his father's
fate. He was one smart rat; one minute he was seen, the
next he had gone like the wind. After his father's demise
he seemed to vow unspeakable revenge and no one could

stop him, least of all the farm workers. He had constructed countless, complicated, zig-zag escape routes, some spiralling downwards only to surface several metres from a large tree that could easily be climbed. He used these when the heat was on and men were closing in to snuff out his life in a surprise attack.

"A rat who has one burrow never lives for long," Konky's father had often said; wise words his son never forgot.

Konky would fill his burrows and holes with all the farm produce he stole.

"You never know when famine will strike," he would reason.

Some of his stashed food items would germinate and grow on the burrow floor due to the lengthy storage time, especially those items near the exit. When famine struck years later most farmers died from starvation and Konky's friends visited him asking for favours. He was often able to help them with his stored surplus.

These days he had to be much more careful with a family of his own to think about. He had chosen a more honourable path in life, reducing his risks, adventurous lifestyle and escapades by half, although he could not afford to give them up entirely, he enjoyed the fun anyway. He always made sure he did not spend two nights in the same burrow, often moving home with his family to ensure their safety. He had worked out how to detect and avoid the human traps.

"No human will love you well enough to freely place food on a platter for you. Be wary and alarmed when you see such a false gesture. I don't want to end up like my father," he would say.

Rodent and Konky had become close friends years before when Rodent would escape the Bakery Rat Community at night and go into the jungle near the rubbish tips in search of extra rations. On one such occasion he had met June,

who happened to be Konky's first cousin. It was Konky
who encouraged the young bachelor to marry June.

"You are all very welcome, my friends, how are you all?
I hope you had a good journey. How are things in the bakery? I hope all is well?" asked Mr Konky without pausing
for breath.

He was quite suspicious of everyone and friendship really did not figure much in his world, nevertheless, he was
happy to receive his cousin and her family. He took his
visitors to where they could leave their luggage and al-
located burrows to everyone, furtively showing them the
exits. June Rodent was all too familiar with the goings-on
in the tough neighbourhood in which she and her siblings
had been brought up. Later they all got together for a family dinner and a quick chat, all well positioned enough to
spot any suspicious attack by an intruder.

That night Mr Rodent and his friend sneaked out to visit
human neighbours' farms, checking out the crops and
helping themselves to what took their fancy. They made
sure they avoided any pitfalls and traps making safety
their watchword and returning early enough to grab a few
hours' rest.

Four days later the Rodent family made the return journey to their home. They reached the River Mungu at the
height of a storm, which buffeted them with howling,
strong winds.

"We have to plunge into the river no matter what, for
we cannot afford to waste another day outside the Bakery
Rat Community. I will jump in first then your mother, just
as we did before. All right?" asked Mr Rodent.

"Yes, Dad," chorused the children.

When they reached halfway across, disaster struck. A
female crocodile, having overheard their conversation,
was determined to get her meal as soon as possible. Before
anyone could say, 'Watch out!' there was a terrific splash
as the hungry predator attacked an inexperienced young

rat. Mr and Mrs Rodent and one son escaped with their lives, but the others were dragged down the River Mangu as food.

Back home safely, they counted their losses and mourned bitterly for their lost children. As if that was not enough to bear, tragedy struck again when Mrs Rodent and their only remaining son died in a trap. That year was a bad one and Mr Rodent always referred to it as a nightmare.

Mr Rodent was still rocking in his chair, lost in thought and almost dozing off, when Mrs Messy scampered in to inform him of how far the planning and preparations had gone for the real day.

Mr Rascal had been one of the few lucky rats who had relocated to the City of Canterbourne with Mayor O'Brien. He was very clever indeed, showing special skills in the art of survival, despite the dramatic change in the fortunes of the O'Brien household.

When things got really bad he started making a meal of Anita's school books, which prompted threats from her to do dreadful things to the culprit on finding him. Rascal was too smart to be caught and knew how to cover his tracks. He was able to remember some of the alphabet lessons he overheard and eventually managed to scratch out the word 'policheaters' when he really meant 'politicians'. He scavenged for any writing materials he could find in the rubbish bins, making the other rats like Mr Rodent and Mr Stewrat wonder what he had in mind.

Mr Stewrat had got his skin burned when he had up-turned a pan full of hot oil that Anita had just finished using to roast the sweet potatoes she took to school in her lunch box. He had mistaken the pan for something else, maybe a pot of honey, and had been lucky to survive to tell the tale. From then on he had learned to be more care-ful when curiosity reared its head, for the accident had left his tail permanently scarred, giving it a somewhat different colour and a crooked shape. He was the rat in the Bakery Rat Community with the shortest tail, other parts of his body were hairless and he was unable to move quickly, but he still had his life.

It was common knowledge in the Bakery Rat Community that when Mr Stewrat, Mrs Messy and Mr Nutty got together it was big news that often made the headlines. The trio were not just a bunch of skilful and ruthless organisers, but mean executors, hell-bent on making their mark in the oncoming war against Mr O'Brien and his people. They were counting the days and keeping a lid on their plans.

Mrs Messy was a notorious diehard who cared nothing for others. She had been with the O'Brien family in the early days at the bakery, leaving her family behind in the Cayon jungle village. As far as she was concerned, the end justified the means no matter how bloody the end turned out to be. She had lied about her husband to settle an old score, so that he had been charged with treason and executed. She openly admitted that she did regret her actions. She was a well known busybody and it was rumoured that nothing happened in the community without her knowing the details first hand.

Fellow rats were weary of her dubious nature, so often gave her a wide berth, worrying if she promised to pay them a visit. They all knew she could not be trusted so some told her of fictitious, month-long important outings with their family or were not at home when she called. They knew that if she stepped over their threshold the whole world would soon know every little family secret, it having been magnified out of all proportion, hence the cold shoulder she was given, which many thought served her right.

At the last supreme rat council meeting, Mrs Messy had been the one who had made a thought-provoking announcement.

"Fellow rat citizens, it has come to our notice that humans have started poisoning our only source of livelihood – our food in the bakery. We could all eat then die in our sleep in our thousands. Fellow rats, listen well. Let it be known to you all that humans are greedy, crafty and extremely selfish. None of them love you enough to wish you well and place food in your homes or in a strategic position for you to eat and stay alive – no way! Fellow rats, don't be fooled, for this food is nothing but a poisoned food trap with only one goal; to eliminate us and send us all to an early grave. I strongly advise that whenever you see this kind of charity, jump over it and find the real thing. Humans would not be stupid enough to poison the heavy sacks of cereals and flour they need, just to kill us. They are far too selfish, so rip open those sacks and eat the contents."

Mrs Messy acknowledged the thunderous applause that greeted her speech, looking from left to right proudly then sitting beside Mr Rodent. She had spoken well for once.

Mr Nutty chatted quietly to Mr Rodent before making his way to the raised platform. Everyone applauded, although he had said nothing, but he was a well known figure in the community. A heavy silence seized the atmosphere as he cleared his throat to begin.

"Fellow rat citizens of this great bakery, I salute you all for your courage to defy the stupid humans and their empty threats by registering your attendance here tonight at this meeting. After major consultation with Mr Rodent, I have been given the go-ahead to set out a modus operandi on how to launch our self-preservation tactics before the real battle begins. This war has to be fought on all fronts. I tell you that the humans are daily making their own plans to decimate us, and to feign ignorance of this would be sheer madness on our part. Mr Stewrat, Mr Rascal and Mrs Messy will work with me on a particular project, the ins and outs of which I am not permitted to divulge now for security reasons, but I know we will all be glad of it

sooner rather than later. Thank you," he said, before scur-
rying back to his seat as everyone clapped wildly.

The meeting ended in the early hours of the morning
with everyone happy that they had attended. Even Mrs
Messy was quite impressed by the outcome, and happy
that things were gradually slipping into a state of madness
– nothing in life made her happier. Gossip would flow like
rivers, there would be much misfortune and she could
hardly conceal her excitement as she hurried to her lonely
home in the bakery behind the massive storeroom doors.

A few months later almost every hidden corner and
floor in the bakery was riddled with rat holes. The burrows
were often interlinked with several emergency escape
routes in case of trouble. Everything had been concealed
perfectly with dried leaves or rotten cereal bags, a massive disguise to make the bakery staff think all was well.
Most rats were shocked and speechless, for no one had a
reasonable explanation – it was the hidden project spoken
about at the meeting. Mrs Messy had kept her mouth shut,
which amazed Mr Stewrat and Mr Rascal.

"Whoever did this must have made a perfect and wise
calculation while we were totally unaware," said a con-
fused rat.

When Mr O'Brien visited the bakery some weeks later
to have a word with his secretary about a business deal,
some rats, whose identity remained shrouded in mystery,
climbing straight through the tyres and into the boot – but
why?

Things moved on apace until news filtered into the
Bakery Rat Community that many rat holes had been
drilled throughout the City of Canterborne with direct access to the bakery. The humans' ground floor rooms, especially pantries and kitchens, were riddled with hidden
holes to the exterior, some even linking up to the nearest
jungle for easy entry and exit in preparation for D-Day.
The rat community came to realise that the extension of

their territory figured in the battle preparation between themselves and the humans.

The humans could not understand the meaning of the holes and some tried to fill them in with dry sand or bits of carpet. Complaints were pouring in to Mayor O'Brien.

Mr Loudmouth was instructed to disseminate information to every adult rat with the message:

"There is a need for a massive increase in the rat population. Every young rat must get married and produce children in fact there is no limit to the number of offspring. As the oncoming battle will boil down to a matter of numbers, the more we are, the stronger the unity."

Mr Loudmouth encouraged everyone to follow his example as he now had over a dozen children and was still expecting more. As days ran into weeks and weeks into months the rat population was ever on the increase. There was no going back for enough was enough – a fight to the finish.

The human citizens of the City of Canterborne were feeling the tension. Complaints were flooding in to the mayor from every quarter, and those humans who had been indifferent at first began to worry over the lack of property and food. Nothing was safe from the rats, everything being eaten and urinated upon. The humans' first reaction was to grab and kill any rat on sight, but that was extremely difficult.

Mr Lotto, a council member and a victim of the rats' onslaught told his story.

"This prompted me to set an iron trap baited with a barbecued piece of fish. Funnily enough, in the early hours of the morning as I strolled into my storeroom... Guess what? Lo and behold, a giant rat was hanging out of the entrance to the trap with its forelimbs clamped together as if begging me to set it free. To me it was good riddance to bad rubbish – the score was settled."

He turned to Mayor O'Brien.

"You should have seen the smile on my face. How the vermin found its way into my securely locked store-room and plundered it was a big mystery I still find hard to comprehend. I just left the rat there with blood on its mouth until the morning, only to find its mates had se-creted the body away to God knows where. I searched but couldn't find it, so reset the trap with more fish for the next victim."

Later that day, news reached the bakery that one of the rats hidden in the mayor's car boot had met his death during a special operation clandestinely planned by Mr Rascal. He had been one of the young talented rats groomed by Mr Rascal and Mr Nutty. He was given a de-cent burial with three days set aside for the community to mourn his demise.

During the proceedings, Manatee, the mayor's wife, suggested using cats, but someone disagreed saying the neighbourhood cats were merely pets, not streetwise enough to master the tricks of the wild. They would ob-viously be no match for the militant rat families that be-lieved in the magic of numbers and multiple attacks on any perceived enemy, a sure target, human or animal. To the human citizens of the City of Canterborne all delibera-tions had to point to the final destruction of the rat popu-lation anywhere they were seen. Total war was declared by the aggrieved citizens, but the use of cats was ruled out as they were pets and had to be protected.

As the meeting was drawing to a close someone spotted a pair of little, shiny black eyes, the eyes of Mr Loudmouth as he hid behind a massive flowerpot in the corner of the room. He had been carried away by the fact that he now had enough information to give Mr Rodent and that the humans' plans would be well studied and countered. Little did he realise that he had overstepped the mark and was no longer concealed in the shadows.

"Look out!" was the shout of someone who had spotted

a ratty figure moving behind the flowerpot.

Before Mr Loudmouth knew what was happening, all hell broke loose as the alarmist pointed in his direction and the mayor's men rushed towards him in a frenzy. I would be mad to wait, he thought, and thundered out into the open to find the nearest escape hole, but his luck ran out as a heavy stampede of humans blocked his exit. He was everyone's target and die he must. No matter how he tried to escape he just could not, then someone smashed his head against the concrete floor and he blacked out. His little head splattered blood and brains everywhere and his remains were later picked up by a human and thrown into a bin. This marked the beginning of their victory over the rats' invasion.

# CHAPTER FIFTEEN

I N THE City of Canterborne the humans were exhausted
with the constant presence of the rats in their numbers,
and their unrivalled destructive tendencies.

"Nowhere is sacred, not even our bedrooms, wardrobes
and chest of drawers where we often keep valuables like
cheque books, bank details and other important items.
The vermin often dare you to your face and get in there by
whatever means, shredding everything they see and leaving behind their droppings to shame you," complained
Mr Lotto.

Complaints such as this were numerous, so something
had to be done urgently to resolve the situation and seal
the fate of the troublesome rats, possibly banishing them
into the jungle where they rightly belonged.

Eventually a meeting was fixed at the City Hall beside
a beautiful monument in the city centre. It was reported
in the newspapers and Mr Rodent quickly sent one of his
trusted spy mice to the mayor's residence to sneak around
and secretly eavesdrop then report back to him.

It was a bright sunny afternoon when the meeting con-
vened. All arrived promptly at exactly 3 o'clock. Mayor
O'Brien walked to the platform to make his opening
speech.

"My good citizens of the City of Canterborne, I feel so

honoured to be given this apportunity to address you all today. We can no longer continue to be indifferent to the dreadful menace of these vermin called rats. We have been pushed to the wall by their nefarious activities in our homes and work places, we can no longer tolerate it, so now it's time for action. I need your suggestions. Thank you."

He stepped back to make way for the next speaker, Mr Hunter, a cabinet member who was true to his name. He never took chances in tackling the rat infestation in his home in fact he had trained his cat to hunt them out. One trusted feline had died minutes after killing and eating a rat that had earlier digested poisoned bait, so now the situation was getting very serious. He was very worried by the rat menace and the enormous increase in the rodent population. He complained that his cats were no longer interested in chasing and killing the rats, so maybe they had sworn an oath of secrecy or allegiance to the rat community.

"Now they attack in their hordes like swarms of flies, maybe 40 rats at a time. You can hardly kill one or two and allow the rest to escape and regroup in larger numbers. I've never come across anything like this before," he confessed.

Mr Hunter added that the use of hot water, by pouring buckets full of it onto the vermin could do the trick of decimating them. He bowed and left the stage.

Mr Lotto, the deputy mayor, suggested purchasing a large consignment of metal rat traps, the ones with sharp teeth. He also thought that the traps should be distributed free of charge to every household for a better result.

"This is bye-bye to the rat menace since no home would be without a rat trap," he said, also suggesting the use of barbecued fish for bait. "Those little thieves love that," he joked.

During the proceedings, Manatee, the mayor's wife,

suggested using cats, but someone disagreed saying the neighbourhood cats were merely pets, not streetwise enough to master the tricks of the wild. They would obviously be no match for the militant rat families that believed in the magic of numbers and multiple attack on any perceived enemy, a sure target, human or animal. To the human citizens of the City of Canterborne all deliberations had to point to the final destruction of the rat population anywhere they were seen. Total war was declared by the aggrieved citizens, but the use of cats was ruled out as they were pets and had to be protected.

As the meeting was drawing to a close someone spotted a pair of little, shiny black eyes, the eyes of Mr Loudmouth as he hid behind a massive flowerpot in the corner of the room. He had been carried away by the fact that he now had enough information to give Mr Rodent and that the humans' plans would be well studied and countered. Little did he realise that he had overstepped the mark and was no longer concealed in the shadows.

"Look out!" was the shout of someone who had spotted a ratty figure moving behind the flowerpot.

Before Mr Loudmouth knew what was happening, all hell broke loose as the alarmist pointed in his direction and the mayor's men rushed towards him in a frenzy. I would be mad to wait, he thought, and thundered out into the open to find the nearest escape hole, but his luck ran out as a heavy stampede of humans blocked his exit. He was everyone's target and die he must. No matter how he tried to escape he just could not, then someone smashed his head against the concrete floor and he blacked out. His little head splattered blood and brains everywhere and his remains were later picked up by a human and thrown into a bin. This marked the beginning of their victory over the rats' invasion.

Back in the Bakery Rat Community, as the weeks went by, everyone was getting anxious as they counted the days to Mr Loudmouth's return and had received no news of his mission. Their worst fears were confirmed when a jungle rat, who had stumbled across the unfortunate rat's remains whilst searching for food in a rubbish bin, eventually, after dealing with an important family matter, broke the news of Mr Loudmouth's death to Mr Rodent. He was shocked and appalled at the demise of one of his trusted aids and within minutes the news had spread, making the rat community more determined to settle the score with 'those bloody humans'.

"Here we go again; another trusted and loyal member gone forever. Fallen prey to humans, not to mention my personal loss," said Mr Rodent.

He ordered all the rats to march into the humans' homes, telling them to be careful and watch out for traps.

"Don't eat anything that looks suspicious, avoid poison, silly cats and metal traps, but vandalise anything in sight. Shred their clothing into rags, spare nothing, and if they try to capture you rip off their bloody fingers – show no mercy. This is our protest, so go off in your thousands, confuse them, let them know this is no game – now is the time for action! If anyone is killed, do not be apprehensive, but continue where others stopped…"

Mr Rodent was still speaking at the general rat council meeting when Mr Rascal and Mr Nutty rushed in as if being pursued by heaven knows what. They both scurried to the raised platform and, after a show of hands, Mr Rascal was waved forwards by Mr Rodent. Mr Rascal bowed slightly in recognition.

"Fellow rat citizens," he thundered, "I give you all the honour and obeisance, for the entire city is now boiling like hot water. I charge you to be extremely careful while on your various missions. You will be leaving in groups of a thousand at a time to enter humans' homes and maim, kill and destroy if need be. Cause them as much grief as they have caused us. Make sure every home is infiltrated, but be careful to take the rat paths and don't ever set foot on the tarred highways with those ridiculous smoking vehicles that pollute our environment. Avoid being spotted and crushed. I warn you that they are taking a very hard line. When you reach the city you'll see various marks showing the burrows we've drilled, which are covered with dry leaves, so just push them aside and make your way into their pantries and kitchens.

Go in there and wreak havoc; take what you can, destroy what you can. They don't stay awake at night like we do, but don't spare them. Avoid the many traps they have set for you, and mind what enters your mouth because it could be your last meal. Use their septic tanks, pipes and gutters as escape routes, and even if they contain water, just swim. To survive this mission you must be prepared to sink or swim. Now check your names on Mr Nutty's lists to find which group you are in," he concluded.

Mr Rodent watched Mr Rascal with secret admiration, thinking how clever he and his friends were to have made such wonderful plans.

The silent battle between the human leaders and rat citizens was passive at first, as the humans believed it was only a matter of time before the entire rat community would be wiped out, but little did they know the rat population of the City of Canterborne. They had no idea of the vast numbers the rats' breeding project had amassed over the years of perceived human cruelty and hatred.

The Bakery Rat Community had persuaded the jungle rats to join forces with them against those who had never hidden their disdain and hatred for the rat citizens. No one could have predicted that the war was so imminent, but most looked upon the death and loss of Mr Loudmouth, one of the rising stars of the rat community, as fuel poured on an already blazing fire, a fire that was now unstoppable.

The first group of one thousand who clandestinely

marched into the city home of Mr Lotto, Mayor O'Brien's deputy, succeeded brilliantly. They left havoc in their wake after having a field day, as the family was away on vacation in Disneyland, Paris. They entered through the drilled burrows linking the rooms to the outside fenced boundary of the house close to their rat path. Some of the rats that returned to give their victory speech had mouthfuls of grain, which was piled up in their numerous underground storerooms for a rainy day.

This unexpectedly easy victory encouraged and boosted the morale of the doubting Thomases in the Bakery Rat Community and further strengthened their resolve to fight humans to the hilt.

Mr Lotto and his family returned a fortnight later to be greeted with the shocking mess their comfortable home had now become. Not even the bedrooms and sheets had been spared, having been urinated and defecated upon by some of the more adventurous young rats. Mr Lotto vowed to have his revenge, but a clear look at the scale of the destruction told him of the vast numbers of rats with which he would be dealing, not just a few. The family would have to make serious plans to get even with those stupid 'villains', as Mrs Lotto referred to the rats, never using the word 'rats'.

Mr Nutty and Mr Rascal often allowed a week to go by between onslaughts, for tension to ease. The next home to be targeted was that of Mr Heartless, the city's minister for health and environment. He had been given the position because of his decisiveness when resolving issues. The rats hated his guts, for he never thought twice about slamming a death sentence on every rat family, and he had been the one to import rat poison to hand out freely to every human family. The previous year, three-quarters of the rat families in Canterborne had been decimated, leaving relatives to mourn their loved ones, hence their resolve to multiply their numbers in readiness for war.

Mr Rascal gathered his group together and, raising his forefinger, started to speak.

"It would be wrong to describe the vulture as tactically aggressive, as it would be wrong to describe the piranha as tactically aggressive. The vulture will flee at the slightest hint of aggression, but red-bellied piranhas will stand up and fight in shoals, making mincemeat of their enemies. In this battle you are the piranhas and should brace yourselves," he concluded.

That night a contingent of 1,000 strong, battle-tested and well-selected rats would storm Mr Heartless's home and give him a dose of his own medicine by wreaking havoc on his property. There was no mistaking that it would be the mother of all battles, as their victim had a reputation for his unbridled hatred of the rats and their activities. He had even suggested to the mayor that if the rats were not eradicated as a matter of urgency there could possibly be an outbreak of plague. This thought made the human leaders more determined to root out the rat population despite the problem of their huge numbers.

"The more you eliminate them, the more they increase and turn nastier," Mayor O'Brien said.

The rat citizens of Canterborne had won their first battle against Mr Lotto, which fired their desire for more adventure.

"We believe Mr Heartless's household will be a pushover, and he can't be exempt no matter whom he thinks he is," said Mr Rascal.

The human citizens of Canterbourne had come to the realisation that the rats were rarely seen during the day, but at night swarmed in their thousands, even millions, like countless termites to heaven knows where. Everyone was on their guard, especially the leaders of the community, as they did not want to experience the fate of Mr Lotto, who was spending a lot of money on repairs, something for which he had not budgeted. Households were keeping night vigils.

"Who knows, it could be your turn tonight. These rats work in mysterious ways keeping their plans a secret," said Mrs O'Brien.

The rats were aware that the humans knew of some of their plans, but kept to the date of the raid on Mr Heartless's home, for he had to be taught a lesson to make him steer clear of the rats and their businesses. Everyone was boiling for action. The battle was to commence at 3 am via the underground burrows, when the humans would be fast asleep.

Mr Heartless vowed never to experience a catastrophe like Mr Lotto's, so made sure someone in the family was always on guard. He knew the rats hated him because of his firebrand policies against them and he felt the same because of their filthiness. He thought they would be imbeciles to enter his home, but little did he know that the attack was imminent.

The Supreme Rat Council, chaired by Mr Rodent, targeted the important human leaders for the raids. These were the people who made the rules that affected rat society, but there were others, the minority of real human leaders, who represented the entire voice of the population.

The rats knew it would be a fight to the finish. Mr Rascal and Mr Nutty had planned everything down to the last detail. They would be attacking the storerooms, kitchen and lounge, just to teach Mr Heartless a lesson. As the minutes ticked by, zero hour approached and the wait seemed endless...

Mr Stewrat had sharpened his teeth in readiness for the attack. He believed that their actions would teach the human leaders to mind their own business, be fair in the use and distribution of the nation's abundant human, material and natural resources for the benefit of all and also to back off and leave the rats in peace to lead their normal lives without fear of intimidation and harassment such as being chased about in the broad day light like a common criminal.

A few days earlier, Mr Nutty and Mr Rascal had sent five able-bodied spy mice into Mr Heartless's roof and other secret places to monitor events in the household. They were strictly warned to stay hidden, but to sneak around when the family was asleep and report their observations, which would then be relayed to Mr Rodent. They often reported directly to Mr Nutty, who was directing the operation. They also had to check for escape routes, and the location of cereals, rice, beans and whatever sacks were bulging with food. If they were discovered it would spell the death knell for the invaders, but if this happened they were to flee for their lives.

"Hopefully, we shall triumph," said Mr Rascal.

At around midnight, Mr Heartless and his wife were in the lounge enjoying a family film and drinks. His wife's head was resting on his chest as they lay on the sofa watching the television. The children were asleep in their bedrooms. Mrs Heartless dozed off and was carried upstairs to bed by her husband, who later returned to the sitting room to finish watching the film. He soon became sleepy and awoke with a start, just managing to drag himself upstairs to bed. It was a little after midnight and the whole house was quiet. Outside, the shrill of the night crickets could be heard as they chorused in unison.

Some hours later the deep silence of the house was disturbed by the rushing sound of hundreds of rats scampering into the residence. Most entered through the myriad of burrows and some through broken sewage pipes. Mr Rascal and Mr Nutty were conspicuous because they were directing operations, dividing the rats into groups that each attacked a particular area of the house. One group went to the kitchen to deal with the contents of the food sacks and bags, one to the pantry, the third group to watch out for Mr and Mrs Heartless and give the signal for all to flee if they came to attack them. The fourth group, led by Mr Nutty, went to the lounge.

The viciousness and ferocity with which the rats attacked the home of Mr Heartless was hard to imagine. Those in the lounge ripped off the sofa covers, gnawing holes in them and littering them with their droppings and urine. The kitchen group stuffed the corners of their mouths with grain and whatever food they could grab. In the pantry, the bags and sacks were being plundered; those stored by Mrs Heartless to be used when current stocks had run out.

The last group on watch for the owners and their children were running around excitedly hoping the situation would last forever. In the course of their running one sighted a mouth-watering menu hanging from a flat-toothed metal contraption, the pleasing aroma so enticing that the three rats went closer to taste the delicacy. They had no idea that it was an alarmed rat trap set by Mr Heartless. Before anyone could blink an eye, the rats had become victims, setting off the alarm and waking up every member of the household.

The Heartless family members each grabbed a club or anything they could use on the rats. Looking down from the top of the stairs, Mr Heartless was shocked to see hundreds of rodents, and wondered if he was dreaming. The reality of the situation soon slapped him in the face when he entered the kitchen to behold a moving sea of rats. He shouted to his children to come and attack the vermin. He had already started clubbing the rats, and around 20 lay dead at his feet. There was absolute uproar as every rodent tried to escape, mostly without success as the Heartless family pounded the unlucky ones.

Escape routes were overcrowded, there had been no warning of the impending danger and chaos reigned. Only about one quarter of the rats who had invaded the house were able to escape unscathed, the remainder perishing in the battle. Mrs Heartless was bitten by a rat she cornered and tried to capture; one from Mr Nutty's specially trained group. As a result, she lost two fingers.

The attack had gone so wrong that even Mr Rascal broke one of his forelimbs and was lucky to have escaped with his life. Mr Nutty was not so lucky; he was spotted trying to wriggle into an overcrowded corner hole in a desperate attempt to escape and was bludgeoned to death with a wine bottle as he queued in the slow-moving line, dying on the spot. Those fortunate enough to have made it home were full of fiery tales of the battle. Mr Rodent listened to them all. Mr Rascal was too injured and in pain from a seriously fractured forelimb to speak, nevertheless, his spirits were high. If nothing else, we have taught Mr Heartless a lesson to henceforth mind his own business, he thought.

Mr Rodent had never expected an easy victory and quickly sent his condolences to the bereaved rat families throughout the Bakery Rat Community.

"It is our price for freedom. We can't have it handed to us on a golden platter, you all know that," he said.

Mr Rascal received treatment at Mr Dokky's rat clinic and was recuperating fast as he planned yet another attack, but for when he had fully recovered.

Mr Dokky was a smart young rat who had been intelligent enough to master the complexities of medicine and treatments. His grandfather had been one of the earliest physicians in the rat community in Cayon village. He had taken the time to encourage and groom his grandson in the art of medicine, having seen his interest. He had learned fast, to the extent that some rat families believed he had become a better doctor than his grandfather, who passed away after a battle with Mr Snake. He had been attacked in his own burrow, the fight lasting for several hours. He was injected with countless shots of lethal snake venom, something his frail old body could not counter. He died in the early hours of the morning with the satisfaction of knowing that his grandson would definitely take up the reins from where he had left off.

Mr Dokky knew the cure for many ailments just by looking for and picking particular herbs. Hundreds of rats were lying in the clinic waiting for treatment – the aftermath of the rats' invasion on the household of Mr Heartless.

News of the invasion reached the Jungle Rat Community. They pledged to lend their support on subsequent occasions, being very happy with their colleagues' exploits.

The entire City of Canterborne was agog by what had happened the previous night in the household of Mr Heartless. It was more a shock than reality to the Heartless family.

"Who would believe that the bloody vermin would dare to visit my home in such a despicable manner?" questioned Mr Heartless. "Wherever the few survivors are now, they will be licking their wounds – I've paid them back in kind," he said, looking at his wife's two missing fingers.

He took his wife to the private hospital to receive the best treatment before ordering his men to clear out the remaining rubbish in his house. Rats' bodies were everywhere, the result of the night's fracas, but they were never counted.

"Just throw them all into the bin, for I intend to show them to Mayor O'Brien and the cabinet members before deciding what to do with them."

Mr Heartless swore to get even with the rats and resolved to visit Mayor O'Brien to discuss how to banish the vermin from the city once and for all. In the days after the battle, Mr Heartless's household harboured some extremely repugnant foul odours, the result of the decomposing rodents. Many rats had died in inaccessible places, so the smell hung in the air then the flies came, attracted by the stench.

He could not visit the mayor as planned because the hospital contacted him to say his wife was critical and his presence was needed as a matter of urgency. By the time he got there she had died from loss of blood and a bad infection that had spread throughout her body, caused by a rat bite. At one point Mr Heartless thought of moving as the house held so many memories of his late wife, also he was finding it increasingly difficult to cope with the plague of flies

When the Hospital Rat Community heard of her demise they were overjoyed and immediately relayed the vital information to Mr Rodent. It was well received in the Bakery Rat Community.

Mayor O'Brien and his family went to pay their respects and vowed to put an end to the rat menace, but little did they know that they could be the next target. The rats had already taken over his staff and bakery, the staff turning a blind eye to the increasing rat population and being so hard worked that they did not have time to listen to the news of the rats' invasion of the City of Canterborne.

After Mrs Heartless's funeral, things were never the same again for her husband, who made up his mind to relocate to another city to start a new life, as there was nothing left for him in Canterborne.

"The rats have eventually exiled me from the city I loved so much," he said, sadly.

A few days later Mr Heartless moved to the City of Kenton a couple of miles away from Canterborne, where he continued his fight against the rats.

Mr Rascal soon recovered the use of his forelimb and regained his health thanks to the careful treatment of Mr Dokky. He was in good shape and fit to stage another attack, but this time he intended to grasp the bull by the horns; he planned to face Mayor O'Brien's household.

"This could be the battle of all battles," he told Mr

Rodent.

Mrs Messy, and Mr Konky from the Jungle Rat Community, were recruited to provide a good number of young, able-bodied citizens for the attack on Mayor O'Brien's household and in fact the entire City of Canterborne. Mr Rodent warned that before an attack took place any wise rat family should relocate to the jungle for safety, since he could not guarantee their safety or his own for that matter.

A concrete alliance was made between the Bakery and Jungle Rat Communities, with the help of Mr Konky and Mr Rodent, who made sure that everything was executed correctly. Mr Konky hated the humans for their pride, greed and self-centredness, so never thought twice about the attack on them, even if it cost him his life, as long as the goal was achieved.

Mr Rodent, Mr Konky, Mr Rascal and Mrs Messy joined forces to train several thousand rats in the art of warfare. They used the Bakery Rat Community playground for their rigorous and endless training, taking time to master all the burrows made by Mr Rascal and the dear-departed Mr Nutty. They climbed trees, swum and learned how to detect bait, rat traps and poison. They made sure their teeth were sharpened, and were schooled in how to bite as many as possible within seconds.

"This bite puts them in check, nick off their fingers – serves them right," Mr Rascal instructed.

As the days went by, plans were matched up with various training exercises.

# CHAPTER SIXTEEN

I N THE City of Canterborne, Mayor O'Brien and the community leaders were putting their heads together on how to forestall another possible rat attack.

Some humans were acquiring cats to boost their arsenal, and were aware that the invaders knew of the presence of baited rat traps, so avoided them like the plague. Some traps had been set for months without catching a single rodent.

"They all seem to have suddenly gone to school to study how to avoid rat traps," said Mrs O'Brien.

"They shouldn't have to wait too long for the surprise of their lives," said Mr Pepper, who had purchased several canes and a large kettle for a large amount of water.

He intended to pour boiling water into the burrows and possibly boil the rats to death.

"It would take a lunatic to think I'm not going to avenge the losses of my commercial goods at the hands of these bloody wicked vermin."

He made sure that no suspicious holes and burrows were left unsealed, especially in the stockroom where daily havoc had been wreaked on his wares by the enemy who often entered through the rafters to scavenge, almost putting him out of business.

Mayor O'Brien ensured everyone that they would have

the last laugh when they sent the vermin back to the jungle where they rightly belonged, being too poor and wretched to live among humans.

Most of Mr Heartless's neighbours, not being able to cope with the foul-smelling situation any longer, had followed suit, relocating for fear of a sudden outbreak of cholera to which no one wanted to fall victim. There was an exodus in the City of Canterborne as health security could no longer be guaranteed.

In the middle of the night, thousands of rats streamed from nowhere, taking up their positions as they scurried out of the burrows. Some marched towards Mayor O'Brien's compound whilst others were evenly distributed and instructed to file into other humans' homes. In the maze of oval heads and black beady eyes it was difficult to determine the leaders, especially with the added number of mercenaries from the Jungle Rat Community.

Those who marched to Mayor O'Brien's home had easy access because of the spy mice permanently stationed there. Burrows had been drilled in the basement, precariously threatening the very foundations of the building, so much so that a strong wind would have probably flatten it. The rats divided into large groups of 200 and scattered into every corner of the house. Mayor O'Brien's family slept peacefully, not knowing that the invaders were within.

The rats going to the kitchen rushed over to a sweet smelling pot of porridge on the gas cooker and, without stopping to think whether it might be poisoned, forcefully dragged the large metal cover off for better access. There was a loud bang as the lid slipped off and fell, hitting the cement floor. The noise awoke every member of the household, who rushed down the stairs only to have the greatest shock of their lives.

They knew it might happen one day, but not so soon and not when they were unprepared. The entire ground floor was swimming with countless rats, so much so that they could not find space to stand. Mayor O'Brien summoned outside help. Once the hunted had learned to hunt the hunter, the hunting game would be no more.

After that night, the mayor purchased five enormous cats. He believed they would terrorise the rat families and decimate them in their numbers, but they were not keen to do so for he kept spoiling them with the tastiest cat food available. At last they sighted a formidable number of rodents and threw in the towel; the cats that could not escape fast enough were severely attacked by the aggressive rats, about 20 to a cat. The mayor lost three of his pet cats and that is when the battle really began.

The neighbours who trooped in to assist in the extermination of the rats became embroiled in much bloodshed, biting, killing, stampeding and crushing. When the going got too tough for the rats, the smart ones started sneaking away into obscurity under cover of darkness. No room was spared by the rats, and Mayor O'Brien was bitten once or twice. No one knew the whereabouts of their leaders, but they could not afford to die, so had given their orders then disappeared, leaving the younger ones to fight.

What was happening at the mayor's house was also taking place in other prominent households in the City of Canterborne.

Many human fingers were bitten off, there was blood shed in the rats' camp, and cats and dogs were maimed, blinded or bitten to death. The pets were up against formidable numbers all at once. Some had succeeded in killing one, two or even three rodents at a time, but they were eventually overwhelmed by the biting rats and gradually bled to death giving the rats their victory.

"Unity is strength," is what Mr Nutty had told the rats, and he had been correct.

"How on earth did we allow these kinds of numbers to go unchecked?" queried the city treasurer. "We overlooked their existence initially, and now they've taken over our beloved city. What shall we do now?"

No one was interested in thinking of what to do, for the situation was out of hand and only a fool would continue to live in such a polluted city, doomed to witness a severe epidemic in a matter of weeks if not days. Dead rodents littered the city and the council had given up any hope of restoring it to its former sanitary glory. The more the men worked, the more the rubbish increased – it seemed endless.

The straw that broke the camel's back was an outbreak of bubonic plague with fleas and flies everywhere in countless numbers. Lives and good health could no longer be guaranteed and people were abandoning the city in droves, especially after the rapid deaths of five major personalities, leaving no one in doubt as to their vulnerability. Mayor O'Brien had lost servants and workers to the plague and now Anita, his daughter, was critically ill.

He had completed arrangements to move to Kenton, where Mr Heartless lived. Just like everyone else, he wasn't staying behind to sort things out, in fact most people believed there was nothing to sort out as the rodents had won and that was it for now.

The situation had been so bad that the rats had devised their own tactical ways to survive. They had wreaked revenge on the wicked and exploitative leaders of the day, and their cronies, who often advised them wrongly for their own selfish gain.

# EPILOGUE

THE AUTHOR has used the following analogies to expose the evil leadership in Africa and Third World countries. This sends a clear message that the entire world is watching and a reminder that it is time for them to get their act together and turn over a new leaf.

The message is for them to be fair to the electorate; those who put them in power. Listen to the voice of the people and fulfil your promises instead of robbing the economy of the poor countries.

The author abhors violence of any sort. He enjoins the masses to follow the path of mutual dialogue and peaceful protest if need be, to resolve issues.

The front cover of the book of a rodent eating an old boot:

- the boot symbolises power, leadership and oppression;
- the rodent symbolises the suffering of poor citizens – the electorate in the City of Canterborne (Africa);
- the bite or attack on the boot is the civilian protest against bad leadership.

Nancia Abdul, Mayor Dakota's Caribbean wife - the

extravagance, rape, exploitation and finally the political downfall of Mayor Dan Dakota.

Junta the dog - the epitome of the agents of oppression employed by the leaders of the day in the City of Canterborne (Africa) to intimidate, exploit and even exterminate their hapless subjects (rats).

Akitu Kuku - the suffering, child labour and fate of the majority of the impoverished children of the City of Canterborne families (African families) at the hands of their leaders regarding their health, well-being and welfare as daily they lose the battle against HIV/AIDS and other common treatable diseases. The latter is on the increase, but the leaders turn a blind eye.

Mr Rodent - the workers' trade union leader, the champion of the causes of the common man (rat), and the true hope of the hopeless in the city. He serves as their eyes, ears and even their minds, often helping to checkmate the wicked political policies and laws affecting them. He actually risks his own life to take the bull by the horns when a situation becomes too unbearable.

Johnny Walkman - the plight of the young, jobless school leavers and graduates (African and Third World youth) of Canterborne (Africa). The Devil finds work for idle hands.

Lord Stephen Kobis - the good and positive influence on Cayon village by using his skill and wealth to create jobs and gainful employment for the jobless. He symbolises a great rising above 'colour and racial prejudice'. Man is man whatever his colour.

Messrs Nutty, Rascal and Stewrat, and Mrs Messy - agents for positive change in Canterborne's (Africa's) society.

Mr Nutty's trance - the daily dreams of the deprived youth in Canterborne (Africa), but unfortunately most of the positive ideas and dreams end up in a shallow forgotten grave in a cemetery.

Humans' iron house on wheels – taxis, and drivers whose vehicles emit fumes that pollute our environment.

Dr Pete O'Kabuka – the positive image and blessings of a Western education. One of the shining stars who soothes the hearts and minds of the downtrodden in Canterborne (Africa) and the surrounding areas.

Storage Rat Communities – a clear reference to locations where oil has been discovered, and abundant scattered resources; for example, gold, coal, gas, diamonds, crude oil, crude barite, uranium deposits, iron ore deposits etc. These are found in large quantities in several parts of Canterborne (Africa) and are exploited by the greed of those in power.

Mayor Dan Dakota's death – his removal from office by the power of the electorate who put him there in the first place. His demise is the regeneration and rebirth of the new government and leadership that will hopefully bring new hope, re-awakening and new policies. The heavy mortar tied around his neck is the long prison sentence for his misjudgement of the nation's resources.

Bubbles Bubbles wine parlour – a market place and spiritual hideout where people go to forget their worries in their flight to a temporary euphoria; a melting pot for the gathering of troubled souls.

Kija cult – a traditional belief that often rules in the primitive African and Third World local judicial system.

Bakery Rat Community – a miniature African state within Canterborne (Africa) - the parent body.

Rodent's son – reference to the 'above the law' attitude of the immediate family members of an incumbent leader.

Mayor O'Brien's election success – change and the manifestation of the will of the electorate over those who run their affairs.

The class struggle in Canterborne was exposed by the trial visits of Mr Nutty and his friends to the City of

Canterborne. The segregation between the rich and the poor: the leaders and the led. The poor and downtrodden were forbidden to visit certain quarters – Government Reserved Areas – but these were built using their sweat and toil.

www.ingramcontent.com/pod-product-compliance
Lightning Source LLC
Chambersburg PA
CBHW051842170626
46807CB00003B/1309